D1587299

St. Teresa's
Hereford
HR1 4AT

THE OLD ROADS

OF

SOUTH HEREFORDSHIRE

Trackway to Turnpike

Heather Hurley

DEDICATION

To my husband, Jon, who shared my enthusiasm exploring the highways and byways of Herefordshire.

'There was once a road through the woods
Before they planted the trees.
It is underneath the coppice and heath,
And the thin anemones.'

Rudyard Kipling
The Way Through the Woods.

© Heather Hurley 1992
ISBN 0 906885 10 8
Published by THE POUND HOUSE,
Newent, Glos, GL18 1PS

CONTENTS

INTRODUCTION

'Travel for pleasure is largely a development of our own time, yet men have journeyed, willy-nilly, as far back as records can take us, driven by greed or piety or lured by the prospect of adventure.'

Jane Oliver

A few years ago I purchased the Ancient Roads of England, written by Jane Oliver in 1936, and this delightful volume inspired me, encouraged by my publisher, David Bick, to tackle local aspects of the same subject. My initial interest in parish paths and the roads of Ross was later extended to South Herefordshire – a charming rural area lying between the cathedral city of Hereford to the north, the Forest of Dean in the south, and bounded east and west by the fruit fields of Much Marcle and the remote hills of the Welsh Borders.

A glimpse at an Ordnance Sheet of South Herefordshire does not immediately show a fascinating network of ancient highways and byways, but closer inspection reveals a web of lines, dots and dashes representing an historical survey of field paths, uneven bridleways, sunken lanes, quiet roads and busy thoroughfares. Many have been lost or replaced by routes more suited to wheeled traffic during the turnpike era. The gradients of original steep and narrow ways can only be appreciated nowadays by walkers, riders and cyclists, for hills are easily negotiated by modern forms of transport.

These routes formed the basis of today's roads and paths. With the help of past and present maps, research and field work, Herefordshire's rich history of roads from scenic ridgeways to twisting turnpikes can be discovered. At the time of publication all available records were examined, but undoubtedly further documentation will add to the story.

Acknowledgements
Finally I wish to extend my thanks to my husband Jon Hurley for his support and encouragement, David Bick, and David Grech for his detailed maps and drawings. Useful assistance has been gratefully received from Sue Hubbard and her staff at the Hereford Record Office, Robin Hill and Carol Robinson at the Hereford City Library and Elizabeth Teizer at Ross Library. Thanks also to the Gloucester Record Office, House of Lords Record Office, the Museums at Hereford and Monmouth, South Herefordshire District Council and Hereford and Worcester County Council.

1 PREHISTORIC AND ROMAN ROADS

'An interesting study for dwellers in the rural districts of Herefordshire consists in tracking and mentally reconstructing its old roads. Many of these go back to the earliest historic population of the island, the Kelts. Before them the origin of these lanes is lost in remote antiquity. They are generally to be found winding along the sides of hills, with perhaps a preference for dipping into the valleys below.'

Rev. M. G. Watkins 1895

The history of roads began when early man made tracks along ridgeways and between iron age camps. In Herefordshire, Alfred Watkins wrote at length in the 1920s about this subject, explaining his radical theories that mounds, moats and mark stones acted as sight lines along which prehistoric man established tracks. He added 'It may be that all the first straight ways were made for trading, for man must have very early had need for necessities, such as salt, flint, and (later) metals, not found in his own district.' Although controversial, Watkin's books still provide a wonderful source of information about ancient routes throughout the county.

A spectacular ridgeway, preserved as a right of way, runs from Woolhope to Yatton along a limestone escarpment known as Marcle and Ridge Hills. At its southern end it skirts the boundary of Oldbury Camp, the site of a sixteen-acre iron age hillfort. A lesser-known one can be explored by car, leading from Pencraig, a familiar craggy point overlooking the river Wye. It follows a straight alignment through Glewstone and its lost chapel, and on to Sellack where the charred remains of the Elizabethan Caradoc Court stands on a much earlier site. Near here, it continues as a public footpath to Foy lying in an isolated loop of the Wye. A description of this route was written by Fosbroke in 1822, though it is now difficult to interpret:

From Hentland there runs a British Trackway to the Meend, thence to Miret, thence to Wilzon, thence to Whitfield, where it falls into the Turnpike road at Pencreck: but probably went further, for the author has been informed, that, in making the present Turnpike road, a way apparently Roman was cut through. The present road from Welsh Newton to the Callow beyond Dewsall, appears to run upon an ancient line.

Linton near Ross could have derived its name from lying on the line of a prehistoric route. In 1928 S. Cooper Neal wrote:

It is naturally difficult to trace the original trackway. Whether the present road along the top of this ridge called Linton Hill is the ancient trackway, or whether it ran along the level below the ridge, I am unable to say, but I am inclined to think that it was on the lower level on the north side. At any rate there are still the remains of a road passing between the Churchyard wall and the Old Priest's House towards the Line Field and Line House. Possibly there were two of them.

Linton Hill is worthy of inspection, for apart from its fine views the restored Talbot's Well makes an interesting discovery.

Hollow ways or sunken roads are often regarded as being of medieval origin, but there is growing evidence that many are of great antiquity. They were created long ago before the use of wheeled vehicles when foot travellers preferred a direct line regardless of steep gradients rather than a longer sinuous route. Numerous hollow ways are encountered whilst exploring the delightful countryside of Herefordshire. An unexpected one of great depth can be followed on foot from the Axe and Cleaver Inn at Much Birch to Little Birch church. Another intriguing sunken road leads from Bollitree Castle at Weston under Penyard to Fiddler's Cross in Linton. It became an early turnpike road in 1749, but because of being 'in many parts narrow and out of Repair' was replaced by a more convenient route. Sadly upon each visit less of the sunken road remains, though officially shown as a footpath.

Attractive features of sunken roads are the variety of their hedgerows. Holly, yew, oak, ash and hazel are festooned with briars and ivy, making mysterious shady tunnels. Knarled roots embrace bare rock sides above a floor of moss covered boulders, perhaps better described by Rev. Watkins in 1895:

Every here and there, too, from the depth of solid rock or pebbles seen on the side of the lane, some notion may be formed of the extreme antiquity of these lanes, where the slow tide of human life has cut its way in the course of ages, much as the rivers of the country have also deepened their channels during the same long centuries.

One such example can be enjoyed at Altbough above Hoarwithy. A walk or ride along this bridleway reminds one of ancient times while descending from Altbough Hill to the banks of the Wriggle Brook near Tresseck.

The cause of sunken lanes is usually attributed to the constant wear and tear of man and animals with heavy rains washing away loose soil

A sunken lane between Wayne Green and the Traveller's Seat, The original road to Abergavenny, see p.42.

and stone. Deep sections often occur on hillsides where excess water flows at its fastest. This was noted by John Clark in his General View of Agriculture (1794):

> The bye-roads are mostly sunk many feet below the surface of the adjoining lands, by the floods having caried away the soil in the course of ages. In such a situation no road can be made good, nor could it be kept so if it were made, because it is always liable to be destroyed by the floods.

It may be considered that some sunken lanes were made deeper by being excavated as a source of accessible stone. Solid rock sides can be investigated at the bottom of an ancient lane, now tarmac, leading from Turkey Tump to the picturesque ruins of Llanwarne's old church. Also at a minor crossroads previously known as Perry Tump in the parish of How Caple.

At the Fordings, beyond the gate an ancient road from Ross to Linton survives as a public footpath, see p. 36. (David Bick)

Hollow ways which have survived are our only ancient monuments still in use thousands of years after their creation. While exploring them we tread on the same paths as our remote ancestors, forming a continuous link with prehistoric times. More immediate action needs to be made by legislation to preserve them for future generations. Even those defined as rights of way are in danger of losing their ancient hedgerows, and having the centuries of wear ploughed out. Other unclaimed lanes are rapidly disappearing.

When the Romans arrived in Herefordshire they discovered a region criss-crossed by paths and tracks. Evidence now suggests that many of the sunken roads were in much the same condition then as we see them today. In 1922 Alfred Watkins wrote 'It is not easy to realise that many British roads were as ancient to the Roman invaders as the Roman remains are to us'.

The Romans developed an extensive road system from 100AD which formed the basis of our present pattern, although many fell into disuse after their departure. In Herefordshire, Roman routes are described at length in publications such as the Transactions of the Woolhope Field Club. Even so, it is often difficult to determine their exact courses, but recent aerial photographs help towards identifying them.

Characteristic features of Roman roads are the agger, a gentle cambered causeway, with kerbs and side ditches, but in South Herefordshire these features have been modified as their construction seems less complex. The local roads were often surfaced with iron-ore slag taken from the extensive industrial site at Ariconium, where excavations have been undertaken on a number of occasions. Archaeologists' investigations are well documented and can be consulted at Hereford or Ross libraries.

Ariconium was only discovered in the late 18th century, and according to an early romantic description of 1827 it was 'reported by tradition to have been destroyed by an earthquake. The extent and limits of its site are at present discernible by a blackness of soil, strikingly different from all around it, which together with the circumstance of their being very few traces of buildings remaining, accord with the tradition'. The site was mentioned in Iter XIII of the Antoine Itinerary, and a route known as the Dean Road is of particular interest. In 1936 A.W. Trotter wrote 'The Dean Road, which originally was paved and kerbed throughout the entire known portion of its course, runs in a northerly direction from Highfield, Lydney, to Mitcheldean, a distance of 10¼ miles. Whether or not the

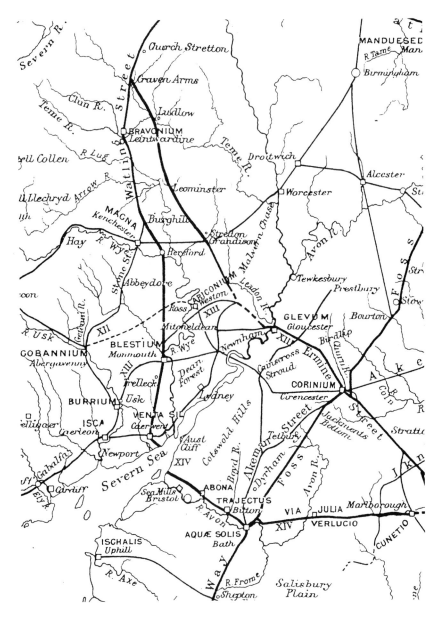

The Roman roads of Herefordshire and the Welsh Borders as recorded in 1903. (WNFC)

road extended beyond the latter place, we have not yet been able to ascertain, but if it did, Ariconium could be its possible — one might say probable — destination'. At Blackpool Bridge south of Soudley an exposed section can be inspected.

A very early route probably used by Romans travelling from Ariconium to Monmouth, was a crossing of the Wye between Walford (Welsh ford) and Goodrich. This important site was later guarded by Goodrich Castle, now a substantial ruin well worth exploring. Although the route continued as a turnpike road from 1749 with its ferry in use until the early 20th century, a section leading to this ancient river-crossing has been unforgivably closed to the public.

Another probable Roman river crossing existed at Red Rail 'road of the ford' at Hoarwithy. The Wye here is deep and narrow, and seems an unlikely site for a ford, but in 1969 excavations provided enough evidence to suggest the course of a minor Roman road, leading from Crossways at How Caple to St. Owens Cross in the parish of Hentland.

A main Roman route was described by Gibbard Jackson in 1935 'The Watling Street is the first of the classic Roman roads. It is indeed a great road, yet hardly so great in length as many a map makes it, nor does it run upon the course which has often been allotted to it. It is

Remains of a Roman milestone in Hereford Museum, found at Magna Castra in 1795. (WNFC)

small wonder that mistakes have been made, and many wrong conclusions arrived at, in connection with this and other Roman roads.' In South Herefordshire, Watling Street followed a course from Hereford, over Callow Hill, past Wormelow Tump and St. Weonards to Monmouth, but no definite traces have been discovered. The present road from Hereford to Monmouth forms part of this Roman route, although its sinuous course suggests an earlier road adapted by the Romans.

Another Roman road crossed the southern part of the county. Known as Stone Street, it led from Magna, the Romano British site at Kenchester, across the Wye and thence over Brampton Hill to Abbeydore. At Madley a lengthy straight section can be followed by car. Roman remains have been identified along this route, and finds from Kenchester include a 3rd century milestone on display at Hereford Museum. Another survival from this period can be seen inside a remote church at Michaelchurch, a Roman altar inscribed 'To the God of the crossroads'.

According to some authorities, an indication of the Roman origin of roads is their retention of the Roman name of street, but others have found this unproven. Street names in South Herefordshire appear at Coughton, Whitchurch, Weston under Penyward, Hope Mansell and Kings Caple.

An exposed section of the Dean Road at Blackpool Bridge.
(John Van Laun)

2 BEFORE THE TURNPIKES

'Scarcely any road between two places is in the best line with respect
to distance and hills. The reason of this is, that the present lines of
roads are the same, except those of roads made of later years, as they
were, when first established by the aboriginal inhabitants of the
country, as footways or horse-tracks.'

Parnell 1833

In the centuries that followed the Romans departure, Saxon
settlements and Norman manors grew and flourished in a land where
travelling was known to be extremely difficult. Changes took place
regarding the importance and use of existing roads owing to
movement of communities, foundation of churches, construction of
castles and establishment of industrial sites. These can be identified by
present-day maps showing routes apparently leading to nowhere, but
where forgotten places can only be discovered by further research and
investigation.

With an increase in travel and transport, pack horse trails, drove
roads and industrial routes were developed. The Pack Saddle Bridge
at Marstow is a reminder of a pack horse trail where a pleasant green
lane leads from the bridge to the site of Marstow's old church.
Demolished in 1856 its only remains are a scattered collection of
weathered tombs standing in a forgotten churchyard. Welsh livestock
were driven along routes through Herefordshire on their way to the
English markets. One drover's road crossed the Wye at Rhydspence
near Hay on Wye, then proceeded along the Golden Valley and hence
towards Gloucester along an undefined course. In 1863 Strong's
Handbook to Ross records a drove road 'which runs through
Brampton Parish was much widened and levelled within the memory
of man; but the continuation of the trackway to Fownhope Church, is
almost in its primitive state, – narrow and centre-worn, and still used
by drovers to avoid toll-bars.'

The Webbs in 1913 recorded 'Thirty thousand black cattle from the
summer and auction fairs of Wales went, every year, in huge herds

through Herefordshire, towards south-east England, choosing, like the Scotch cattle, the bye-lanes in order to avoid the turnpike tolls.'

Trading and industrial routes included limestone ways which are easily recognised by their wayside remains of crumbling lime-kilns. Half hidden beneath years of undergrowth, these can be found alongside public paths in the parishes of Little Dewchurch, Sollers Hope, Fownhope, Woolhope and Whitchurch. Forest of Dean

A pack horse, an early form of transport, from Samuel Smiles'
Lives of the Engineers.

timber, coal and stone were conveyed to Ross along a rough and stoney track called Puckeridge Lane, leading from Deep Dean to Ross through a gap between the hills of Penyard and Chase. This was a turnpike road till 1791 when it continued as a Team road until its closure in 1820. Now down-graded to the status of public footpath it makes an unusual approach into Ross-on-Wye.

As Christianity spread, monastic ways, church paths and corpse-ways were established. Corpseways are rare, but existed where the dead were carried from church to a distant burial ground. At Hentland, a lost lane called Bierless, led across fields from the church to David's Burial Place near Harewood End. In 1829 local landowners found the 'public highway' to be 'useless and unnecessary' so the Justices of the Peace deemed it to be stopped up. One and a half miles north of this church stands Llanfrother, a solitary farm, said to be built on the remains of a 6th century monastic college founded by St. Dubricius. From here a sunken lane descends to Hoarwithy, where on misty mornings one can imagine shadowy monks quietly tackling their tasks. A Monk's Walk at Much Marcle leads from the church to Hellens, a manor house founded by French monks in the 11th century.

Towards the end of the 1500s, carriages came into greater use and from 1784 a mail service started. At this time many of the existing highways were only sunken lanes too narrow for wheeled vehicles, so improvements were urgently required, and undertaken by the newly formed Turnpike Trusts from the late 17th century.

Before the setting up of Trusts, road maintenance was carried out by individual parishes under the terms of the 1555 Highway Act, which transferred responsibility from manors to parishes. This is illustrated by parish records. At Hentland the churchwarden's accounts of 1688 record a William Mynd being paid 'for mending the highways', and at Upton Bishop an agreement made in 1683 'for repairing ye highways' was signed by 23 parishioners.

An appointed surveyor inspected and reported road conditions, then organised statute labour to perform any necessary repairs. The system proved unpopular and ineffective, and some parishes had insufficient resources to maintain long stretches of busy highways. Occasionally they were aided by public subscriptions or private individuals who provided funds for road and bridge repairs.

In Ross-on-Wye, its famous benefactor, John Kyrle (1637–1724), the 'Man of Ross', raised by public subscription sufficient funds to restore a 14th century causeway leading from the foot of Dock Pitch, now Wye Street, across meadows to Wilton bridge, which was built in 1597 to replace a former ford and ferry crossing. The completion of the causeway was commemorated by a pillar bearing an inscription 'At this spot was cheerfully begun what is now happily completed, the labour of this Causeway, winding in the parishes of Ross and Bridstow, hence to the Black Pool Bridge, and thence in a connected line to Lady Pool arch'. The pillar had disappeared by 1827, but a causeway still exists. Over the years it has been altered, especially since 1833 when Ross Turnpike Trust constructed a road from the town to the bridge in order to avoid Wye Street's steep gradient.

In 1639 Roger Lechmere of Fownhope Court left a small legacy towards the cost of repairing Mordiford bridge. This fine 14th century stone construction spans the river Lugg shortly before it joins the Wye. The bridge remains as an attractive and interesting feature in this picturesque village, and still manages to cope with today's heavy traffic.

Sixteenth and 17th century documents are a useful guide to road descriptions and locations. In 1580 a written survey was made of the Pengethley estate at Sellack. It reveals some intriguing references — 'part of common way leading to Monmouth', 'between the Kings Highway', and 'way from Abergavenny to Ross', all of which survive as public roads or paths. An Indenture dated 1652 mentions 'the way leading from Caple Street towards Red Rayle', now a discontinued route from Kings Caple to an ancient crossing of the Wye.

Brief descriptions of Herefordshire's roads appear in writings of the pre-turnpike age. 'The descent is as long and steep in some places as its riseing' is a comment made by Celia Fiennes who travelled through England and Wales during the reign of William and Mary. Daniel Defoe in his Tour through the whole island of Great Britain in the 1720s remarks on the 'badness of the roads', but despite this 'great quantities of cyder are sent to London, even by land carriage tho' so very remote'.

Attempts at making the Wye navigable had never been successful. Since the reign of Edward the Confessor the river had been used, but it was not till 1662 that a serious effort was made to establish the Wye as a commercial waterway. This and later schemes were unable to tame its swift waters, sudden floods and shallows.

With the expansion of London and its foreign trade, political and agricultural changes plus the growth of industries, Herefordshire's narrow lanes became inadequate. They were impenetrable and

Above: *The Wye Bridge, Hereford, from an old print. It was constructed in 1490 to replace a 12th century timber structure.*

Below: *Wilton Bridge, erected shortly after an Act of 1597. (Ross Old Book and Print Shop)*

impassable, churned into mud by horses hooves and deeply rutted by wheeled vehicles. John Webb in his book of the Civil War refers to the 'wretched state of roads ... overhung by trees, the mire of January was hardly dry at Midsummer; in other places the bare rock, worn into inequalities by heavy rains, rose at ascents in ledges like stairs.'

These remarks are still applicable to a number of routes. At the time of writing, a former road leads from the Crown Inn at Whitchurch to Marstow but is obstructed by fallen trees, and its future as a right of way is in jeopardy owing to a missing footbridge across the replacement road constructed by Hereford Turnpike Trust in 1820. At Ballingham beyond the Cottage of Content Inn, a sunken lane is totally obscured by years of overgrowth. It is a public footpath but was formerly an 18th century turnpike leading from Hereford to Hoarwithy Passage.

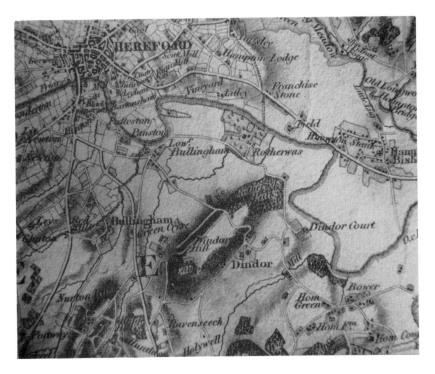

A detail from Henry Price's map of 1817, showing the old road across Dinedor Hill, see p.56

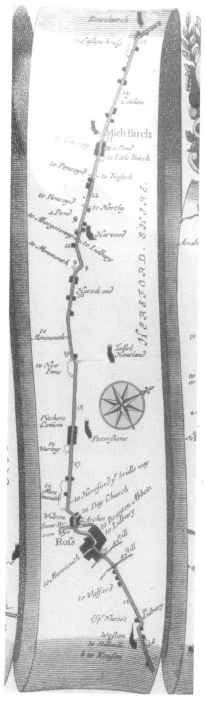

At the turn of the 18th century even more pack horses, cumbersome wagons, trader's carts, carriages and droves of livestock were using the badly neglected and narrow roads of Herefordshire. It is not surprising that the method adopted to cope with this problem was the setting up of Turnpike Trusts. The system was established in 1663 to improve the New Great North Road in the counties of Cambridge, Hertford and Huntingdon, but it was not till the 1750s that it had spread throughout the country. In its infancy, most Trusts did little more than adapt existing roads, but real improvements gradually took place, and at the peak of the turnpike system in the early 19th century many bold new stretches of highways were constructed, which are still in use today.

Left: *A section of the Ross to Hereford road in 1675 from Ogilby's strip map, see p.70.*

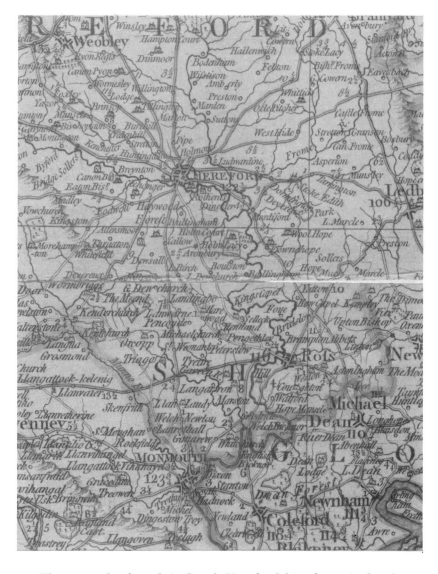

The network of roads in South Herefordshire from Andrew's map of 1786, slightly enlarged. See p.42.

3 TURNPIKE TRUSTS

'It is owing to the turnpike system of road management that England is so superior to other countries with respect to her public roads.'
Parnell 1833

Acts of Parliament were required to establish Turnpike Trusts, making them responsible for maintaining a designated network of highways. Payment in the form of tolls was collected from road users, which was spent on improving the roads. The name is derived from an early method of placing a long pike across a road to stop traffic; when the toll was paid the pike was turned, hence 'turnpike'.

In 1726 a comparatively early Turnpike Act was passed for 'Repairing and Widening the Roads from the City of Gloucester to the City of Hereford.' Apart from Ledbury this was the first of a series of Acts relating to Herefordshire. Trustees were empowered to erect gates or turnpikes, receive tolls, choose collectors, appoint surveyors, mortgage tolls, demand statute labour and elect new trustees. Repairs, improvements and amendments were legally undertaken on roads which were measured by milestones, as directed by the Act. Individual Road Acts allowed tolls to be collected for a term of twenty one years, which was considered sufficient time for putting the roads in good order. The system seldom succeeded; many trusts fell into financial difficulties, and thus continual requests were made to renew or amend Road Acts during the turnpike era.

Local men of substance were appointed as trustees, and up to 100 or more names suggest that this number was needed to assist the passing of an Act. Many proved to be indifferent with only a few actively involved. Most were less knowledgeable than the previous parish authorities, and others who subscribed to the venture expected to be repaid. Amongst the trustees named in the Gloucester and Hereford Road Act of 1726 were such notables as Sir Hungerford Hoskyns, Herbert Ruddall Westphaling, James Walwyn, Thomas Symonds, Robert Minors, Vandervoart Kyrle, Francis Woodhouse, William Merrick and William Gwyn Vaughan, together with the Mayor and Aldermen of Hereford.

The 1726 Act dealt with two routes leading from Gloucester to Hereford. One closely followed the present A40 to Ross joining the A49 to Hereford, and the other branched off at Lea along the course of the B4224 through Fownhope. The Act stated that 'by reason of the many heavy Loads and Carriages, Coaches, Passengers, and Droves of Cattle, which frequently pass the said Roads, and also by means of the Narrowness in some Places thereof, the said Roads are become very bad, ruinous, and almost impassable'. It seemed that the turnpiking of these roads was the only acceptable method to effect repairs, although there was no adequate technology or experienced road builders until the next century.

Milestones erected by the Turnpike Trusts still provide a familiar feature standing alongside former tolls roads. Usually marked on Ordnance Survey maps, these reminders of the past can be easily located, but their condition varies from careful preservation to total neglect. Although difficult to date, early ones can be inspected between Callow and Hereford on the A49 and along the A466 between Welsh Newton and St. Weonards which was turnpiked in 1769. There is an elaborate milestone at the Traveller's Seat near Skenfrith. Here a weathered stone dated 1780 stands at a forgotten crossroads, where main routes converged before the Welsh trusts amended the roads at a later date. Slightly outside the area covered by this book, but worthy

The Travellers Seat Milestone
—now nearly illegible and overgrown with ivy.

of inspection on the Hereford to Worcester road at Withington, stands a five foot shaft of a wayside cross. Since 1700 it has been used as a milestone directing travellers to Hereford, Ledbury, Leominster and Worcester.

Gates, bars and toll houses were carefully sited at crossroads and junctions to catch a maximum amount of tolls from travellers. Near the gate stood a toll house, either purpose-built, converted from a cottage, or just a wooden shack where the collector lived. Toll houses of this period can be seen at Lea Line and Wilton. Much altered, they lie along former lengths of highway which were later realigned. An interesting document of 1795 records the sale of the old road and toll house at Wilton, after a new road was constructed to avoid an inconvenient stretch between Wilton bridge and the Primary School at Bridstow.

A feature of each toll house was its board displaying a long and complicated table of tolls varying under subsequent Acts. The amount depended on the number of horses or oxen drawing a vehicle, whether horses, asses or mules were laden or unladen; the width of wagon wheels were also taken into account. All livestock were charged by the score and double tolls were introduced during winter and on Sundays. Exemptions were allowed for vehicles carrying road-mending materials, soldiers on duty, conveyors of mail, churchgoers on Sundays and carriages on election days.

Instead of appointing toll collectors the trustees often let tolls for rent or offered them for sale by auction. This is illustrated in an Indenture of 1795 made between eleven Ross Trustees and an innholder from Mitcheldean 'to let or farm by the year the Tolls to be taken at all or any of the Turnpikes ... to the said Joseph Hales who was the best Bidder for the same Term of three Years ... at the yearly Rent or Sum of nine hundred and fifteen pounds payable by equal monthly payments ... and hath this day given Security to the Satisfaction of the said Trustees.'

The paying of tolls annoyed some road users and often led to hostility. Riots occurred at Gloucester, Over, Lea, Ledbury and Hereford in the 1730s. Quarter Sessions relate that armed rioters 'Came to the Lea Turnpike' which they 'Cutt down and Destroy'd' and so terrified the keepers that 'they will not ask, nor Demand any Toll'. Similar outrageous behaviour took place in Gloucester in 1734 when 'a multitude of men, disguis'd and arm'd with guns, pistols, and swords, did between the hours of five and six this morning in an indolent and riotous manner enter the town, crying out Blood for Blood, and Down with the Turnpikes, threatening immediate death to any who should dare oppose their licentious proceedings.'

These exciting events did not deter the expansion of the turnpike system in and around the county of Herefordshire. By the mid 18th century Hereford and Ross had established their own trusts, followed by Monmouth in 1755, Crickhowell in 1772 with the Forest of Dean in 1796 and Newent in 1802. Curiously Ledbury formed its own trust earlier than most in 1721. This extensive turnpiking in the Wye and Severn valleys suggest a growth in traffic which the existing roads together with the waterways were unable to cope with. This partly led to the formation of the Hereford and Gloucester Canal in 1791, but because of delays and difficulties it did not reach Hereford till 1845, only a few years before the railway arrived.

Hereford parted from Gloucester forming its own trust in 1730, turnpiking an extensive network including the roads 'leading from the several Gates and Bridges of the said City', 'the great Roads leading into South Wales', 'to the Town of Monmouth' and 'to the Town of

A woman in a market cart paying toll in 1807 (W. H. Pyne).

Anno vicesimo secundo

Georgii II. Regis.

An Act for repairing and widening the several Roads leading into the Town of *Ross* in the County of *Hereford*.

Hereas the several Roads here- Preamble. in after-mentioned and describ- ed, that is to say, the Road leading from the Town of Rofs in the County of Hereford, to Harwood's Inn, being Five Miles, or thereabouts; and al- fo the several Parts of the Road leading from the said Town of Rofs towards the Ci- ty of Gloucefter (which lie in the said County of Hereford) being Five Miles, or thereabouts; and also the Road lead- ing from the Town of Rofs aforefaid, to Hoarwithy, be- ing Four Miles, or thereabouts; and also the Road lead- ing from a Place called the Town Brook, in the Town of Rofs aforefaid, to a Place called the Perry Tump in the Parish of How Caple in the said County of Hereford, being Four Miles, or thereabouts; and also the Road leading from the Town Brook aforefaid, to a Place called the Smith's Shop, in the Parish of Much Marcle, in the said County of Hereford, being Five Miles, or there-

6 U 2   abouts;

The first Ross Turnpike Road Act of 1749.

Ross'. Their 'ruinous and Bad' condition made them 'impassable in the Winter Season' and 'dangerous to Travellers'. The atrocious state of the roads prompted certain landowners and business men in Ross to establish a trust in 1749. Eleven routes were turnpiked radiating from Ross and covering a total of forty-three miles.

The trustees of both towns were continually pressing to enlarge their terms and powers during the 18th and 19th centuries, resulting in further Acts being passed for Hereford in 1749, 1769, 1789, 1810, 1819 and 1835 with Ross following in 1773, 1791, 1815 and 1862. Together these two trusts extended, widened, repaired, amended and improved the roads in south Herefordshire. A heavier usage was reflected in the amount of tolls collected. Hereford Trust received £1558 in 1781 increasing to £4262 in 1820, and £7031 in 1843 before falling to £6281 in 1862.

By the early 19th century, Hereford and Ross were surrounded by turnpikes, making it impossible to enter without paying a toll. An exception occurred in Ross after 1815 when the turnpike road from Brampton Abbotts was discontinued and its toll-bar removed allowing free access into the town. Rare survivors from the turnpike days are toll tickets given as proof that payment was received. One issued at Walford in 1856 exempted travellers from paying again at 'Pencraig, Corpse-cross and Coughton Gates, and two tickets clear the district'. Anyone caught evading a toll were fined by the trustees as set out in the relevant Road Act.

Avoiding paying tolls was another issue dealt with by the trustees. An occurrence in 1847 was recorded in the Ross Turnpike Trust Minute Book 'A Chain to be placed at Dung Pits because of evasion at Corpse Cross'. Again in 1848 there was another mention 'the useless and unnecessary mail coaches evading the tolls', which provoked the trustees into sending a memo to the Postmaster General.

The Minute Book provides an interesting and rare insight into the meetings of the Ross Trust held at Barretts Royal Hotel. Its activities were administered by a few keen and concientious trustees who dealt with many items from the major tasks of improving, repairing and

Opposite
Above: *The old road and toll cottage at Wilton, in use before 1795, see p.23. (Heather Hurley)*
Below: *A typical 19th century toll house at Huntley, on the road from Ross to Gloucester. (David Bick)*

providing new roads, maintaining toll houses and gates, to financial complexities. Other entries record the problems of weighing machines, removal of encroachments and transportation of road-mending materials. Surveyors, foremen and contractors were hired and fired, and because of drinking it became necessary for the 'Foremen of roads to pay their workmen at own house and not on any account at public house or beer house'.

Apart from his normal duties, in 1843 the Ross Surveyor was ordered to 'inquire of every Pound Keeper in the Ross District of Turnpike Roads what cattle, horses, sheep or pigs have within the last two years been impounded . . . and what funds have been paid by the owners in their being released'. A restored village pound stands alongside the former turnpike road at Walford. Another surveyor in 1851 was obliged to employ a man at a shilling a week to prevent waggoners from obstructing the road at Wilton. A notice announced 'that all waggoners or other persons staying in Wilton for refreshments for themselves or their horses are required to draw up their waggons or carts as near as conveniently may be on the south side of the turnpike road and on that side only − any waggoners or other persons offending against this notice will be prosecuted.'

This colourful account of the Ross Trust provides additional proof that the trustees undertook their duties with responsibility and carried out considerable improvements. But throughout the kingdom there was often disatisfaction and a lack of confidence in the turnpike system. Long-distance travel had become easier and quicker, but locally the turnpikes were unpopular as shown in this publication of 1863: 'The rude expedient of raising a few pence at a time by shutting a Gate in a traveller's way, and detaining him till he has paid the demand, is both expensive and inconvenient.' Nevertheless no better system had yet been introduced.

4 THE TOLL ROADS

'Through the unwearied Industry and increasing Opulence of the Inhabitants of this Kingdom, the Roads in every Part of it are made so convenient for Travelling, that they are the Admiration of Foreigners, and the Pride of the Natives.'

Daniel Paterson 1778

Since their establishment in the early 18th century South Herefordshire's turnpike roads were extensively altered and improved under the terms of each Road Act. With the help of maps and plans of the 18th and 19th century it is easy to locate the toll roads used as mail and coaching routes, but some difficulty is encountered in tracing various cross-country roads. Most exciting is the discovery of abandoned lanes and discontinued routes which provide a realistic impression of original toll roads.

By the mid 1800s many local turnpike roads had undergone major alterations due to the influence of Thomas Telford and his team who surveyed the South Wales Mail Road through Herefordshire in 1824. His plans together with other surveyor's proposals were partly carried out during a very active period of road building between 1815 and 1836.

Most of these proposals concentrated on reorganising the roads around Ross, whose future as a town of the mail coach route had been in jeopardy since innkeepers from rival towns had promoted alternative roads in order to improve their own trade. This problem was settled in 1825 by the Postmaster General in his report on the South Wales Mail Road.

This chapter will endeavour to explain, record and describe a fascinating network of toll roads through South Herefordshire, pointing out numerous alterations undertaken by Hereford and Ross Trusts during the turnpike era. These sites can be explored by car or foot where a right of way still exits.

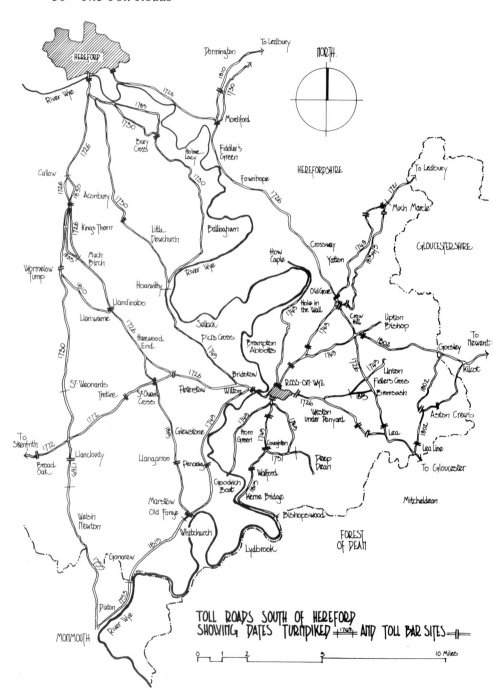

TOLL ROADS SOUTH OF HEREFORD SHOWING DATES TURNPIKED 1749 AND TOLL BAR SITES

The Gloucester Roads

The routes which now serve as the A40 and A49 from Hereford to Gloucester through Ross-on-Wye formed the most important road to London. Already well established by the 17th century it became one of the first to be turnpiked by the Gloucester and Hereford Trust in 1726. In 1730 it was administered by the Hereford Trust to Harewood End, and from here to Lea by the Ross Trust after 1749.

From the county boundary at Lea this road has undergone extensive improvement and widening schemes. This makes it difficult to visualise it as a former toll road, but where realignment has taken place original sections have been left untouched. One such stretch can be traced on the map between a former toll house on the Newent – Mitcheldean road at Lea Line and Knightshill, where a very steep descent was replaced by the present line. Another worth investigating leads from the Crown Inn at Lea, along a partly metalled track to Castle End. These, together with alterations at Hownhall, were completed by 1842.

The original route from Ross to Gloucester at Lea, before Telford's improvements. (Heather Hurley)

Before reaching Ross the road was realigned at Ryford Chapel in 1830 and at Lower Weston in the 1820s. George Strong relates the altered situation of Weston Hall which 'lies a little back from the road, in one of those sheltered spots of which our forefathers were so fond, about 2 miles from Ross: and in consequence of the diversion of the Highway from the North to its Southern side, which was effected more than 40 years ago, it is approached at a great disadvantage.'

At Ross-on-Wye the former toll road went through the Chase grounds, along Old Gloucester Road, then known as Hatter's or Arthur's Lane, past the Market House of 1660 and steeply down Wye Street, formerly called Dock Pitch. This route changed after Road Acts of 1781 and 1815 pressed for: 'keeping in Repair, certain Streets or Highways within the said Town', which 'owing to the great Number of heavy laden Carriages daily passing through the same, are of late become greatly out of Repair; and a certain Turning at the Corner of Hatter's Lane aforesaid is narrow and unsafe for Travellers.'

However it was not until 1825 that the present Gloucester road was constructed, possibly due to the fact that in 1821 King George IV's journey from Ireland to London was delayed by vehicles obstructing the old road, as described in the Ross Gazette of 1891:

He entered the town by the old Wilton road and Dock Pitch (then the only way), and after a change of horses, and taking a glass of wine that was handed to him by Mrs. Mary Howells, the landlady of the King's Head, much to the disappointment of the inhabitants, he drew down the blinds of the coach, intending to hurry on as quickly as possible. Greatly to his disgust, however, on arriving at the Nag's Head, an unexpected obstacle barred his progress for a time. The carrier's waggon had arrived, and before unloading, the horses had been taken out. The place was so narrow that the King was obliged to wait while the horses were brought out again, and the waggon moved out of his way.

This incident led to a great improvement of the town, as shortly afterwards notice was sent from London that, unless a better way was made through the town, the mail would be taken off the road, in consequence of which the present Gloucester-road was constructed.

In 1833 Thomas Telford's plans were adopted as recorded by Dr. Strong: 'Upon the west side of the town there was but one road, and that dangerously steep – down the Dock Pitch. But, in 1830, by forming a sweep immediately beneath the Prospect Cliffs, a more gentle descent was gained.' The large quantity of sandstone cut away

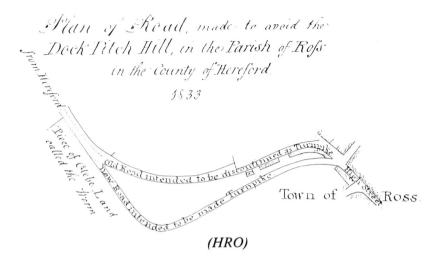

Plan of Road, made to avoid the Dock Pitch Hill, in the Parish of Ross in the County of Hereford. 1833

(HRO)

from these cliffs to form the new Wilton Road, was presumably used to construct the mock gothic walls and round tower built in the picturesque style. This striking entrance to Ross-on-Wye was completed in 1838 with the building of the Royal Hotel.

From Wilton bridge, the toll road made a circuitous route through this hamlet before its realignment in 1795. A surviving stretch of road to investigate leads from the Old Toll Cottage at Wilton along a narrow lane towards the modern Ross Spur road. It originally continued from here to Bridstow school, but its route can only be traced on a map.

From Bridstow to Hereford the only major alterations were carried out after the Hereford Road Act of 1835. Nearly a three mile length of the present road was constructed to replace a difficult and dangerous route across the slopes of Aconbury and Callow hills. This former route now serves as minor roads through Kingsthorne and past Callow church; it then proceeds towards Hereford passing two well preserved mile-stones with iron inserts, 'To Hereford 3 miles', and 'To Hereford 2 miles'. At Hereford travellers paid their toll at St. Martin's turnpike before crossing the Wye bridge of 1490.

Another route turnpiked by the Gloucester and Hereford Trust in 1726 led from Castle End at Lea to Hereford along the line of the present B4224. This sixteen mile stretch, supposed to be Roman, was transferred to the Hereford Trust in 1730, and formed their longest length to maintain. It remains following an unaltered course from

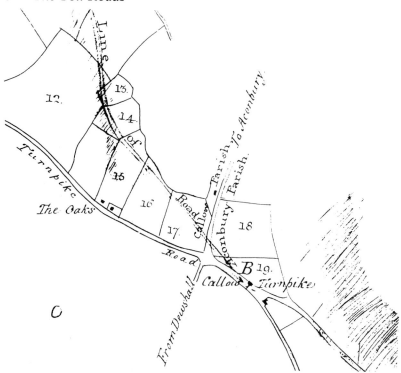

*An 1834 plan of the proposed new line of turnpike road
at Callow. (HRO)*

Castle End over ancient crossroads at Bromsash, Crow Hill, Old Gore, Crossways, Fownhope and Mordiford, where the road bears left to cross the river Lugg over a 14th century bridge before reaching Hampton Bishop and Hereford at the site of St. Owen's toll gate.

In 1781 the Hereford Trustees allotted a sum of £80 to be spent on this road from 'Top of Eigne Hill to the Mill at Mordiford', and from 'Mordiford to Fownhope'. Today travellers from Gloucester to Hereford will appreciate this quieter and pleasing alternative to busier roads.

In 1749 the Ross Trust turnpiked a road 'leading from the said Town of Ross by Weston's Cott, to Linton's Church, being four Miles or thereabouts'. It branched out from the Ross to Gloucester road at Lower Weston and followed an ancient route to Linton. It is still a public right of way and can be explored by following a tarmac lane from Lower Weston to Bollitree with its 18th century mock castle,

A 19th century cast-iron milepost just east of Fownhope.
(David Bick)

then along a footpath closely hugging the remains of a deeply sunken lane to Fiddler's Cross. From here a narrow tarmac lane leads to The Fording, a pretty place where the Rudhall brook is crossed by a stone arched bridge. A footpath sign indicates the way ahead, where the redundant toll road steeply ascends to Linton. Its rocky bottom sunken with age tinkles to the sound of running water instead of iron-shod hooves and waggon wheels. After 1791 a minor alteration was made, but it was not till the 1815 Act that this inconvenient road was abandoned in favour of an easier one leading from the Weston Cross Inn. It was a shorter route as it terminated at Bromsash, and can be investigated by car.

The last two routes included in this section led from Ross to the Forest of Dean. They initially shared the same road through the turnpike at Copse Cross, where the thatched toll house still survives. Before reaching Tudorville the roads divided, one gently following the Wye Valley, the other along a rugged route to Deep Dean. Both were turnpiked in 1749 by the Ross Trust. The first went along the line of the present B4228 'by Coughton's Chapel to a Place called the Quern, in the parish of Walford', later known as Kerne. Using Taylor's map of 1754 it is possible to locate the site of this lost chapel and a place mysteriously called Dead Woman, where the Vine Tree Inn now stands. On Bryant's map of 1835 numerous toll-bars and side gates are shown at Tudorville, Coughton and Walford which made it impossible to enter Ross from this direction without paying.

Under the terms of the 1815 Road Act this turnpike road was extended by 2607 yards from the Quern to William Partridge's Iron Furnace at Bishopswood. It was described as being 'much travelled and used but is narrow, inconvenient, and in bad Condition'. The expense of this improvement is set out as follows:

	£	s	d
To widen and form the said Road	80	0	0
Raising breaking and laying stone for same	137	0	0
Halling materials for same	173	0	0
Fencing the same	64	4	6
Purchase of land for same	100	0	0
	£554	4	6

After the extension to Bishopswood new roads were suggested in 1822 and 1824, which would have affected this turnpike road and influenced the future network around Ross-on-Wye. The proposals were to build a new road between Old Forge at Goodrich to join the Gloucester road at Lea or Huntley, bypassing Ross by crossing the Wye below Goodrich Castle. They were not carried out, but an event that altered the importance of this route was the building of Kerne bridge. An Act of 1825 was for 'building a Bridge over the River Wye, at a place called The Kerne', and for making an 'Approach to the said Bridge, from the Turnpike road leading from the Town of Ross'. The toll bridge was completed in 1828 and formed an important link between Herefordshire and the Forest of Dean. An interesting consequence was the construction of a dry arch to carry the Welsh Bicknor road across a deep rock cutting at Goodrich.

Approaching Hereford from Ross in 1800. (HRO)

The other road from Ross towards the Forest of Dean ran along Puckeridge Lane. The original route climbed up a holloway to Hill Farm, and between the hills of Chase and Penyard to Coughton valley, then along a sunken track to reach a tiny settlement at Deep Dean. In 1820 it was officially stopped up after Justices of the Peace had inspected Puckeridge Lane and found it 'unnecessary'. Luckily the whole route has survived as a public footpath and provides a good example of an early turnpike road.

Puckeridge Lane was discontinued as a toll road in 1791 when a gentler route 'through Coughton Street to Dib Dean' was found to be more convenient. Now known as Deep Dean it lies hidden below the wooded slopes of Howle Hill, and can be reached by car from Coughton. At Deep Dean an irresistible network of tracks connect scanty remains of lime-kilns, pits and quarries, which serve as a reminder that brick and lime were once manufactured in this area.

The Monmouth Roads

The early turnpike roads leading from Hereford and Ross into South Wales do not appear to have followed any straight-forward routes. Perhaps travellers chose the least impassable highways, which in 1756 were 'in a founderous, dangerous Manner'. Eighteenth century maps certainly show a confused network of roads, which were finally supplanted when the Hereford Trust built a superb road to Old Forge in 1819.

In 1730 routes were turnpiked by the Hereford Trust to Pontrilas, Bredwardine and Peterchurch, which at that time were the 'great Roads leading into South Wales'. These lead through the delightful Golden Valley and provide an exciting area of roads to be recorded and researched. Another 'The Great Road to the Town of Monmouth' shared the same highway through Callow as the Hereford to Gloucester road. Beyond Callow it branched off towards Monmouth closely following the line of the present A466. Originally it was only turnpiked to St. Weonards, but a latter Act of 1769 extended the route to Llancloudy Hill due to the road being 'very ruinous, and almost impassable for Travellers and Carriages, and cannot be widened and effectually repaired without the Aid of Parliament'. From 'the Smith's Shop at the Bottom of Llanllawdy Hill' the remainder of the road was administered by the Monmouth Trust from 1755.

Further Acts amended this road and defined its termination at

Llancloudy Hill, which had previously been described as 'vague and uncertain'. Then at the beginning of the 19th century plans were made to build a road connecting St. Weonards to Ganarew and Whitchurch. This was not carried out, but a minor alteration was undertaken at Welsh Newton in 1820; these plans can be inspected in the Quarter Session Rolls.

Today an interesting car journey may be enjoyed along this route. Stopping at St. Weonards to explore a steep sided motte lying between the road and the church, we can then investigate the area around Trippenkennet. Here, an unexplained place called 'Pike Fields' lies a

Milestones and Posts found along the roads to Monmouth.

little distant from the present road, and a distinctive milestone will be found beside Trippenkennet bridge. At Welsh Newton a section of old road will be seen when visiting its 13th century church, where Herefordshire's own saint, John Kemble, lies buried in an attractive graveyard. The road then continues through a steep-sided valley to reach Monmouth, where a typical toll house survives at Monkgate.

Another important road turnpiked was the ancient route from Ross to Monmouth, which crossed the Wye at Goodrich. It was in 1749 that the newly formed Ross Trust turnpiked a two mile length of road to Goodrich Boat, forming the shortest of its eleven routes. The distance is in fact three miles as shown on Taylor's map of 1754 and still marked by three worn and weathered milestones.

From the turnpike at Copse Cross this toll road followed the line of the present minor route to Hom Green, where a wayside cross lies hidden in private woods opposite the church. This nondescript building of 1905 replaced a medieval church, with the 'Cross in the Wood' being its only remains. From here the road passes between the elegant 17th century Hill Court and the picturesque Old Hill Court. Beyond, the present road bears left to Walford, but the former toll road led ahead to the riverside. At this delightful setting, below the rugged ruins of Goodrich Castle, are the remains of a boat house and a half-buried milestone, originally inscribed '3 miles to Ross, 1 mile to Cross Keys'.

Goodrich Castle was built by the Normans to defend this important crossing of the Wye, from which Walford derives its name 'Welsh Ford'. The crossing with 'its bustling life and incessant passing to and fro' in the 18th century began to decline after the building of Kerne bridge in 1828. Despite this, the road continued as a turnpike route with Ross Trustees proposing 'widening and improvement of Goodrich Boat Road near entrance to Hill House' in 1850. Sadly, after centuries of use and continual documentation, stretches of road have now been closed to the public. However, it was never officially closed and attempts to restore its former status as a right of way are being pursued.

Nowadays the major route to Monmouth from Ross-on-Wye is along the A40, reconstructed as a dual-carriageway in 1960. It is the only road in the book that has undergone such a dramatic change since its days as a toll road. Ross, Hereford and Monmouth Trusts were all responsible for turnpiking various lengths of the route. The piece 'leading from the said Town of Ross by Glewston's Tenders, to the

Old Forge' was first turnpiked in 1749, followed by 'the Road leading from Monnow Bridge aforesaid, to the further end of the Parish of Gan y rew' in 1755, which left a section between Old Forge and Ganarew, finally taken over by the Hereford Trust in 1819.

In Thomas Telford's 1824 survey of the area, he proposed various improvements to 'avoid steep inclinations, obtain a more direct, and of course shorten the line'. He reported 'the material is good limestone, procured in the vicinity; in some parts the surface was rutted and rough, and the fences high, but generally the Road is in a pretty good state'. Alterations were carried out at this period, and then the road remained unchanged until its rebuilding in this century.

From Ross, this toll road shared the same route towards Hereford as far as Wilton turnpike; here it branched left through Weirend, Glewstone, Pencraig and Goodrich Cross to Old Forge. Although completely replaced by the modern highway, several sections of old road remain to be investigated. Try following a pleasant riverside path from Wilton to Weirend and Glewstone where stretches of former road can be identified below the embankments of the A40. A surprisingly attractive site, previously known as Glewston's Tenders or Stenders, is where barges loaded and unloaded timber and stone in the 1840s. At that time the isolated cottage was 'Glewstone Boat Beer House and Garden', well appointed for travellers using the toll road and the river crossing.

Other sections of the original route now serve as minor roads leading from Old Forge, through Whitchurch and up to Crocker's Ash before reaching the war memorial at Ganarew. Here it followed the banks of the Wye to Dixton, where an ancient church sits prettily between the river and the old road. Its approach into Monmouth was altered after the Road Act of 1831 for a 'new line of Road from and out of the Turnpike Road leading from Ross to Monmouth, to commence at or near the Entrance of a Lane nearly opposite Dixton Church, leading from the said last-mentioned Turnpike Road towards Manstone's Cross, and to be continued in a Line so as to avoid the Liability to Floods from the River Wye, and to terminate at or in the present Turnpike Road near the Top of Monnow Street'. The earlier route can be followed along Old Dixton Road where a former toll house now stands.

Included in this section of roads to Monmouth is an unlikely long distance route from Crickhowell in South Wales to Ross. It approached Herefordshire 'over Skenfrith Bridge, Broad Oak Green, and to the Cross Hands beyond the New Inn in the Turnpike Road leading from the City of Hereford to the Town of Ross'. The 1772 Road Act also turnpiked a route through the Golden Valley from Welsh Newton 'over Broad Oak Green, through Garway, Kentchurch, Ponttrylass, Ewys-Harrold, and to Ponttanast, in the Parish of Cluddock'. The roads were 'in a very ruinous Condition, and in many Parts narrow and incommodious'.

Although shown as a main route to Crickhowell on John Andrew's map of 1786, it actually followed a maze of lanes until alterations were undertaken by the trustees from Ross, Monmouth, Crickhowell, Abergavenny and Grosmont. By 1833 the road was clearly defined 'commencing at a Place called the Old Turnpike otherwise Cross Hands, on the Turnpike Road from Ross to Hereford, by Tretire, Langunnoc, Broad Oak, Southwell Arms, Darren Bridge, Skenfrith, Norton, Trebella, Kefnycraig, Blaenlymon Bridge, and terminating at Cross Ash in the Turnpike Road to Abergavenny'. This forms the course of the present B4521.

The road from St. Owen's Cross to Skenfrith is a scenic route to explore. Extensive views of the Welsh Borders are impressive as the road meanders past small settlements, and jumps over stone bridges across the Gamber, Llantywaun and Darren brooks. A grander structure of 1824 leads over the Monnnow to Skenfrith, idyllically placed on the banks of the river below a backcloth of rolling hills. Its ruined Norman castle, 13th century church and working mill are all worthy of inspection. Amongst St. Bridget's wealth of historic objects hangs a map depicting the roads and rivers of Skenfrith at the time of Henry VIII.

From here, the original toll road can be explored by following a description written by a local landowner in 1926 'The high road from Ross to Abergavenny then went through the village, passed the Brink and about at Norton's Cross, where it joined the road from Grosmont and so up the steep hill to Cross Vane'. He added 'The present road from the Bell Inn in Skenfrith was made to connect these two in 1820, and so the original high road is now only a narrow rose-tangled lane'.

Before leaving Skenfrith follow a lane from the Bell Inn leading to Crossways and onto the Travellers Seat, where a unique milestone dated 1780 will be found at the start of an abandoned route to Wayne Green. Between Skenfrith and Old Pike a series of later mileposts can still be identified with the help of a 2½ inch Ordnance Survey sheet, a mileometer and sharp eyes. This quiet road is ideal for this purpose

A charming cartouche. The proposals were never carried out, see p37. (HRO)

where six posts have been listed by the South Herefordshire District Council who date them as mid or late 18th century. At the time of writing only five were located – at Southwell Court, Broad oak, Three Ashes, Tretire and St. Owen's Cross.

Another route linking two roads leading from Hereford to Monmouth and Ross was turnpiked by the Road Act of 1810. It started from 'a Place called Windmill Hill near Harewood, through the Parishes of Llanenabo, Llanwarne and Much Birch, to a Place called Wormelow Tump'. From here it continued into the Golden Valley forming today's B4348 to Hay-on-Wye.

The present road leads from Llandinabo, where a pretty church waits to be discovered in the grounds of Llandinabo Court. The original road from Windmill Hill followed a line that can be traced on a map, which joined the present road at a sharp turn before bypassing Llanwarne with its ruins of a Norman church. It then proceeds past Turkey Tump where a sadly neglected 19th century chapel stands. From here it runs alongside an infant brook which rises at Gamber Head and joins the Hereford to Monmouth highway at Wormelow Tump.

By 1842 the old length of road had been abandoned, and a 'Toll House' erected by the Hereford Trust stood at Llandinabo. In Hereford Museum a toll ticket can be inspected, dated '12 day of April 1846' listing 'Llandinabo' as one of Hereford Trust's forty gates. Another three were located in the 'Whitchurch and Llangarron District of Turnpike Roads'.

The final road in this section also happens to be the last one turnpiked in South Herefordshire by the Hereford Trust. It was a purpose-built toll road cutting across a tangled web of lanes forming the present line of the A4137, and it remains as a tribute to the road builders of the 1820s. Considerable finance must have been required, but a Turnpike Trust Return dated 1820 records 'No Sum has yet been borrowed'.

Why this road was needed remains a mystery, since adequate routes were already established between Hereford and Monmouth, and it was built too early to connect with Telford's proposals through Old Forge. Amongst the documents relating to this road is a detailed plan of 1818, and the Hereford Road Act of 1819 for:

'making and maintaining a New Road to lead out of the present Turnpike Road going from *Hereford* to *Ross*, at a Place called the *Tuft*

Wood, in the Parish of *Hentland* in the said County, through the several Parishes of *Hentland, Selleck, Peterflow, Langarren, Marstow, Whitchurch*, and *Goodrich*, into the Highway leading from *Monmouth* to *Ross*, and unto the Rivers *Wye* and *Garron*, near a Place called the *Old Forge*, and through the Parish of *Whitchurch* in the said County of *Hereford*, to the Confines of the Parish of *Ganerew* in the said County of *Hereford*, as a Third District of the said roads, will be of great public Utility:'

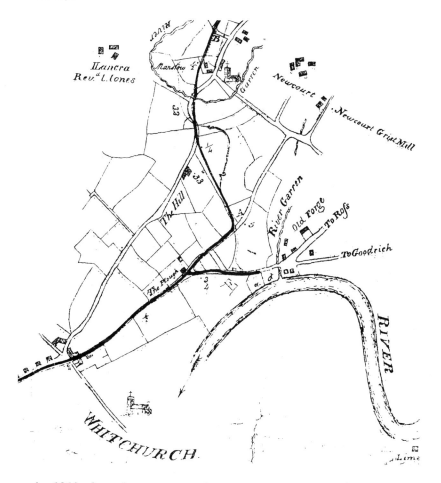

An 1818 plan of a new turnpike road, replacing an inconvenient route through Marstow and over The Hill. (HRO)

At Hentland the construction of this road 'obliterated' an ancient earthwork at Gaer Cop. John Webb wrote in his almost illegible scrawl 'When, modern road – was made (in my time) from New Inn towards Hereford – a part of vallum – there I think in a rough uncultivated state of the past – was cut thro', it was said that a no. of antique horse-shoes were found. The road lay curiously around this'. A narrow curved lane leading to Michaelchurch forms the southern rampart of the hillfort.

From Gaer Cop the road continues past the New Inn at St. Owen's Cross where a former toll house stood, this being one of three gates named in 1846 as 'Old Forge, New Inn and Burnt House' in the Whitchurch and Llangarron District of turnpike roads. Along a level stretch several well preserved milestones may be seen. One at Biddlestone is listed by the District Council and described as 'early 19th century, painted sandstone block with rounded head, bearing inscription To Monmouth VIII miles'. At Burnthouse a dwelling called Stop Gates is a reminder of another toll bar.

Although shown as a 14th century route on Rees's map of 1922, this road between Marstow and Old Forge did not exist until major alterations and improvements were carried out in 1820 by the Hereford Trust. They constructed a fine stone bridge and long causeway supported by buttresses across the Garron and its water meadows. This structure can be admired from the banks of the brook. The road then proceeds through a deep cutting before descending to the third toll gate at Old Forge. This section replaced an earlier road which turned sharply into Marstow, past its former church and across the Garron. From here it steeply ascended to Hill Farm along an old lane to the Crown Inn at Whitchurch. The route has been preserved as a public footpath, but is impassable at the time of writing due to fallen trees and a missing 'Dry Arch' which bridged the cutting over the turnpike road. Unfortunately the bridge was demolished by a heavy goods vehicle a few years ago and has not been replaced by the County Council who report that 'there are plans for the path'. Best approached from the Crown Inn, this old road may be explored by the able-bodied, who might be tempted to scramble over horizontal trees. Their ivy-clad trunks and overgrown wayside quarries now make undisturbed habitats for wildlife.

The Stone Causeway at Marstow Across the Garron Meadows.

The Ledbury Road

At the beginning of the 19th century, Ledbury was described as 'an ancient well-built market town, situated on a declivity near the south end of the Malvern Hills, about one mile from the river Leddon, which it derives its name. It chiefly consists of two streets, which cross each other at right angles'. At that time it appears to have been isolated from south Herefordshire, although attempts to improve its communications had been made in 1721, when it became the first town in the county to turnpike its roads. One route led to 'Stoakes-Court in the Parish of Stoke Edith' where the remainder of the road to Hereford was turnpiked by the Hereford trust in 1730. After various alterations it now forms the A438.

In 1749, the Ross Trust turnpiked a road from 'the Town Brook, to a Place called the Smith's Shop, in the Parish of Much Marcle', which connected with an existing toll road from there to Ledbury. This formed the only route turnpiked between Ross and Ledbury. It proved inadequate until a realignment in the 1830s was built 'to avoid Perrystone Hill and other Steeps in the Township of Yatton', as follows.

From the 'Town Brook' at 'the termination of Brook-end-street' in

Ross, the route took the line of the present Ledbury road, which before the construction of the modern Ross Spur, led to the Blackhouse, now known as the Traveller's Rest. It continued from here to Old Gore where a former inn, smithy and toll house stood around a wayside cross, re-used as a war memorial. Between Ross and Old Gore, toll gates were erected by the Ross Trustees. Those recorded at Townbrook and Perrystone in 1828 were moved to Over-ross and Gatsford at a later period. A toll ticket issued at 'Over-ross Gate' in 1836 can be seen at Gloucester Record Office.

From Old Gore the former toll road may be followed along a quiet country route, up Perrystone Hill and through Yatton with its early Victorian chapel. From here, it continues past Upper House and the imposing Welsh Court to Bodenham Bank, where the original entrance to Homme House is located. Now in the parish of Much Marcle, the road proceeds past Weston's Cider Mill to the Walwyn Arms Inn. In 1828 this route was described by Charles Heath – 'On leaving Ross, we peruse the Ledbury (a fine turnpike) road, for four miles, till we arrive at the Old Goar Inn, at the foot of the hill, where the traveller's will alight, and ascend the higher ground, by the pleasant foot path, that runs parallel with the carriage way below'.

By 1825 this road was considered to be 'annoying to Travellers', and a new improved line 'long in contemplation' would be of 'great Public Utility'. It was reported to the Ross Trustees that '4 Horses in a Team will do the work of 5 in ascending these steeps, and in a like proportion in the Draft of all other Carriages'. Also it would 'open a short direct communication from South Wales, Monmouth, and Ross – to Ledbury, Gloucester, Birmingham and the North – nearer by many miles than any other Road – and will be the means of establishing Stage Coaches to run upon the Line, which these hills now prevent'. A plan was submitted eight years later for a new 'Turnpike Road between the Towns of Ross and Ledbury'; it was completed at the end of the 1830s, and formed the route of the present A449. The new road started from near Coppice Farm, following exaggerated contours around Coldborough, where a purpose-built 'Pike House' still stands. From here it continues circuitiously to Much Marcle, keeping a comfortable distance from Homme House and the parish church. The earlier toll road is joined at the Walwyn Arms Inn, near a pretty black and white dwelling named 'Toll House Cottage'.

While exploring these roads around Much Marcle, do allow time to investigate Yatton's Norman chapel, sample Weston's cider and visit

Hellens, a Jacobean manor house where the Walwyn family lived. Edward Walwyn was a Justice of the Peace, the Parish Surveyor, a trustee for Ledbury and Ross Trusts, and much involved with the building of the new turnpike road. Much Marcle church may be approached by an alternative route. From the old toll road, follow a signed footpath across the fields to the later road, nearby a fine milestone is worth inspecting before continuing ahead to the church. Its graveyard, with the remains of Mortimer's Castle, overlooks pleasant parkland belonging to Homme House, home of the Kyrle's, also associated with the Turnpike Trusts.

Another route, turnpiked in 1749 by the Ross Trust, led off the Ledbury road 'by the Black House, to Upton's Church'. The fascinating Black House stood near the site now occupied by the Traveller's Rest Inn. Ross Tithe Map records a 'House Homestead & Smithy' here in 1840, but the present inn displays a short romantised

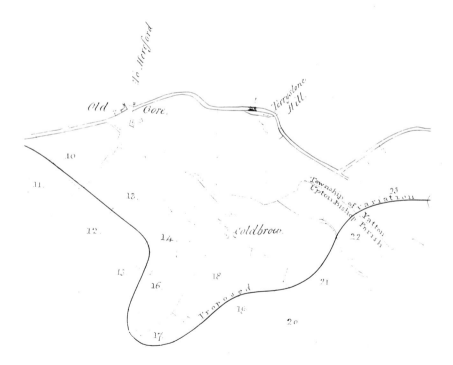

Part of an 1833 plan of a proposed variation of the turnpike road between Ross and Much Marcle to avoid Perrystone Hill. (HRO)

Bryant's map of 1835 showing the former toll road from Ross to Perry Tump.

history, and connects its original name with dying. The legend suggests that the premises supplied biers, hired mourners and provided sin eaters at local funerals. This ancient custom was already obsolete, when described by Fosbroke in 1833. 'In the county of Hereford was an old custom at funerals to hire poor people, who were to take upon them the sinnes of the party deceased. One of them (he was a long leane, ugly, lamentable poor rascal) I remember lived in a cottage on Rosse highway'.

From the Traveller's Rest at the junction of the M50 a minor road leads to Phocle Green, where in 1791 'certain small Pieces of Road leading from the present Turnpike Road at Focle's Green to Crow Hill' were realigned. Two meadows alongside the road were named 'adjoining new road' on Upton Bishop's tithe map of 1839. The earlier route can be followed between clusters of cottages at Phocle Green. The route continues to ancient cross-roads at Crow Hill, where the former toll road terminated after the 1791 Act. At the beginning of the next century Newent Trust erected a toll gate here when they turnpiked a route to Crow Hill. Toll tickets from the 1840 period are preserved at Gloucester Record Office. From Crow Hill a narrowing road winds through Upton Crews to Upton Bishop church, where its solid 13th century tower makes a prominent landmark. An interesting history of the parish was written by the Rev. Havergal in 1883, where he records the cost of 7s 6d in 1824 for 'hauling seats for the church from Ross and Two Turnpikes'.

Almost last in this section, is a road from Ross to 'Perry Tump in the Parish of How Caple', turnpiked in 1749 by the Ross Trustees. In 1773 it was shortened to terminate at 'Cat's Green' in Brampton Abbotts, when the Road Act of that Year stated that 'Tolls collected upon some of the Branches or Parts of the said Roads are not sufficient for the necessary Repairs thereof, and it would be for the Benefit of the Several Persons residing near and travelling the said Roads if the Trustees were to be exempted from the Expence of repairing those Roads, and if the Tolls now payable thereon were to cease'. By 1815 this route had been abandoned as a toll road, and a turnpike at 'Townsend' was removed in 1830. These events led to the establishment of a toll free way into Ross, much appreciated by local farmers and drovers.

This route can be explored by car or on foot using a modern map, but it is interesting to follow on Bryant's map of 1835, which highlights some intriguing places, otherwise missed. Brampton Street is followed from Ross past 'Springfield', at that time the home of James Wallace Richard Hall, a Ross solicitor, banker, turnpike trustee and benefactor. The road now crosses over the Ross Spur, but continues along a stretch where a raised footway makes an attractive feature of the past. At Brampton Abbotts it meanders between farms, houses and cottages to arrive at 'Cat's Green'. From here the former toll road made its way around buildings at Hill of Eaton and steeply descended to the Wye. The river was crossed by a ford before the erection of the present footbridge. Below the 'Site of Tump' recorded as an L-shaped earthwork, the road reaches Hole-in-the-Wall at Foy. The 'Site of Castle' marked here was described in 1858 as 'a formidable and strongly fortified castle, which was demolished in the time of the feudal wars'. An unfenced road follows the riverside through a timeless scene to 'Perry Tump' at How Caple.

Studying an Ordnance Survey sheet, it appears that this road in pre-turnpike times followed a straighter course along sunken paths towards How Caple, which now remain as public rights of way. Hole-in-the-Wall is a walker's delight, where several inviting footpaths lead through this beautiful part of the Wye Valley. In severe weather conditions this rustic route becomes impassable; snow drifts into its deep valleys and its lower levels are susceptible to floods, so it is understandable that it was abandoned as a toll road.

Not to be overlooked is a short 'Branch Road' turnpiked in 1730 by the Hereford Trust, who measured the route as '2 miles' in 1820 and altered the distance to '1 Mile 7 Fur 154 Yards' in 1844. It led from Mordiford to join the Hereford to Ledbury highway at Dormington, which was turnpiked to Stoke Edith in 1730, where the remainder of the route was already turnpiked by the Ledbury Trust in 1721.

The Hereford Road Act of 1810 clearly outlined the route of this toll road 'from the village of Mordiford in the County of Hereford, through the several Parishes of Mordiford and Dormington, in the said County, to a Place called the Cross Hand in the Parish of Dormington, on the Road towards Ledbury'. The new road ran below an earlier route traced on late 18th or early 19th century maps, and used before the Mordiford Inclosure Acts of 1801 & 1809, which had the 'Power to alter or discontinue Roads through inclosed lands'. From Old Sufton this old road runs through Prior's Frome with its inn and attractive collection of dwellings, and at Dormington a right of way leads to a Norman church standing in a picturesque graveyard. The countryside here is aptly described by Thornhill-Timmins in 1892 'amidst deep narrow glens rough with copsewood, where the bluebells are thick as a carpet, and belated primroses take heart of grace to catch the last of spring-time. After a stiff climb we come upon the breezy, gorse-clad shoulder of the hill above a sequested little nook which shelters the old house of Sufton, a manor held during many centuries by the present Hereford family, by the service of presenting to the king a pair of gilt spurs each time it should please his majesty to ride over Mordiford Bridge'.

This family served as Turnpike Trustees together with the Foleys from Stoke Edith.

Hoarwithy Passage and Newent Roads

A lesser group of toll roads led from Hereford and Ross to Hoarwithy, where an ancient crossing over the Wye was known as Hoarwithy Passage until replaced by a bridge in 1857. The horse ferry here was in use when the Hereford Trust turnpiked two roads terminating at 'Hoar Withy Passage, through Holme lacey and Aconbury' in 1730. The routes were not clearly defined until the 1810 Act which described each road separately.

Firstly, the Aconbury route remains almost unaltered since first turnpiked in the 18th century. From Hereford a quiet scenic road leads through Bullingham and Dinedor to Aconbury, where a newly erected sign directs visitors to its historic church, originally attached to a 13th century Augustinian Nunnery. From this 'romantic' place nestling below Aconbury Hill, the road proceeds to Little Dewchurch, offering splendid views of Ross and the Wye Valley before a steep descent to Hoarwithy. Here, an unusual Italian-style church of the 1880s dominates this pretty hamlet, and the River Wye is now crossed by a modern bridge of 1990. A former toll house provides a link with the first bridge built in 1857 by the Hoarwithy Bridge Company.

A toll gate or bar was recorded at Aconbury in 1801, 1819, 1831, 1835 and 1846 on maps and documents. One dated 1801 is a monthly account of tolls paid by James Hereford Esq. for his waggons and horses. Near the site of 'Aconbury Gate' is a stretch of sunken old road in Wallbrook Wood. Now forgotten and overgrown, it can be inspected from the present road and was probably realigned after the 1789 Act 'for making and keeping in Repair, the Roads from the said City of Hereford to Hoarwithy Passage'.

From Hoarwithy the continuation of this road to Ross was turn-

AN ESTIMATE

OF THE

Expence of Maintaining the Hereford Turnpike Trust,

IN THE COUNTY OF HEREFORD,

Between the first day of January and the thirty-first day of December, 1844.

	£.	s.	d.
Manual Labour			
Team Labour and Carriage			
Materials delivered on the Road, exclusive of Carriage	4950	0	0
Damage done in obtaining Materials			
Tradesmen's Bills	250	0	0
Land Purchased	0	0	0
Salaries	440	0	0
Law Charges	50	0	0
Interest of Debt	553	10	0
Watering the Roads	0	0	0
Lighting ditto	50	0	0
Incidental Expences	70	0	0
	6363	10	0

MAIN ROADS.	LENGTH.			DESCRIPTION OF MATERIALS.	QUANTITY of Materials IN YARDS.	PRICE PER YARD.
	Miles.	Fur.	Yards.			s. d.
Abergavenny	11	7	86			
Bromyard	9	4	47			
Hay	11	0	199			
Leominster	7	2	95			
Ledbury	6	3	153	Lime Stone	8700	4 10
Monmouth	11	7	27			
Old Gore	15	7	53			
Sugwas	3	2	10	Gravel and Pebbles	4700	2 10
Length of Main Roads	77	3	10			
BRANCH ROADS.				Blue Rock Stone	1600	3 0
Froome's Hill	11	2	174			
Gorsty Common	2	4	0			
Hoarwithy	7	6	138	Grey Sand Stone	1000	3 0
Holm Lacey	6	0	0			
Ivy Cottage	3	0	0			
Kington	8	0	69			
Little Mansell	2	0	0	Damage in obtaining Materials, Twopence		
Madley	12	3	208	per Yard, average.		
Moor of Bodenham	6	4	0			
Much Dewchurch	12	0	0			
Ross	4	5	75			
Stretford Bridge	9	1	100	Date of the existing Act of Parliament—		
Sufton	1	7	154	June, 12, 1835.		
Turkey Tump	2	1	56			
Weobley	9	2	132			
Length of Branch Roads	99	0	6			
Ditto of Main Roads	77	3	10			
Total Length of Trust	176	3	16			

(HRO)

piked by their trust in 1749. Its course has hardly altered since Taylor produced his map in 1754, but the places have changed. 'Red Rail Ford' was discontinued last century and the roads leading to this river crossing were unofficially closed. 'Caradoc', an Elizabethan mansion was mysteriously burnt to a skeleton in 1986, and the inn at the 'Lough Pool' has recently been extended and modernised. A war memorial now stands at 'Pricks Cross' where a mark stone was recorded by Alfred Watkins in 1828, when he wrote 'I can give one cross place-name which affords absolute proof that the name comes from a stone at a cross-roads, and not from a structural cross. This is Pict's Cross. It was Pricker's and Prick's Cross on 18th century maps, and Pig's Cross on the 1832 Ord. Map'. At Bridstow a mill no longer exists at 'Pool Mill', but the name persists. A little further on the route joins the Hereford to Ross road.

Throughout the centuries the Hoarwithy road has made an attractive alternative between Hereford and Ross despite its series of steep ascents. It is marked by Ogilby in 1675 'to Hereford ye bridle way', shown by Paterson in 1787 on his Itinerary of Direct Roads, and appears on all later maps. Car drivers of today will appreciate the same delights, despite an increase in traffic, as described in an early motorists's guide 'You drive here between dewy meadows where meek looking cattle with red bodies and innocent white faces cease chewing in sheer surprise to stare as you pass. There are masses of cider-orchards, dimpled with green and red-streaked fruit; as you motor along the river-watered central plain you see everywhere steep-sided hills, rising skywards, with woods mantling the slopes from foot to crest'.

The second road turnpiked to Hoarwithy Passage originally followed an unknown route. Only a brief description was given in the 1730 Act 'from the said City to Hoar Withy Passage, through Holme Lacey' being 'Six Miles or thereabouts'. More information is gained from the Act of 1789 for a 'new road to Hoarwithy-Passage' through

'Lower Bullinghope, Rotherwas, Dinedor, Holme Lacey, Ballingham, Little Dewchurch and Hentland', which included 'Part of the said Road, now leading from the said city of Hereford through the said Township of Lower Bullinghope over Dinedor-Hill, through the Parish of Dinedor, is dangerous and inconvenient to Passengers and Carriages on Account of the Ascent and Descent of the said Hill, and it would be more commodious and convenient to make a new Road through the Townships of Lower Bullinghope and Rotherwas, and the Parish of Dinedor, to join the present Road, at or near a Place called Bury Cross'.

These vital clues together with past and present maps help to identify the route of this former toll road from Hereford to Barry's Cross, and its earlier way over Dinedor Hill, where an old road is still visible but not scheduled as a right of way. This road continues to Holme Lacey with its magnificent mansion, built by the Scudamores in the 17th century, and overlooks an attractive stretch of the Wye. No longer required for a country estate, the house currently lies silent and redundant until its future is decided. Pleasant paths through delightful parkland, provide a closer glimpse.

Other places around Holme Lacey are of interest. They include remains of the Hereford, Ross, Gloucester Railway constructed in 1855, the site of 'Even Pitts Ferry' replaced by the 'Fownhope and Holme Lacey Bridge' in 1857 and an isolated church, the only survivor of a deserted medieval village. A cottage at Barry's Cross once served as a toll house, and a 19th century mile post records a distance of five miles to Hereford.

Sometime between 1835 and 1844 the road now the B4399 ceased as a turnpike route beyond Holme Lacey. As a result, its continuation from here to Hoarwithy presents a problem. The route used today around Ballingham Hill only emerged as a through road at the beginning of this century. From a network of roads leading across a range of hills, the 18th century road probably followed a route shown on the maps of Taylor and Cary which ran alongside Tump Farm before continuing straight up Kidley Hill. From the top of the hill to Carey a right of way has been preserved, although no evidence of a former road is visible along the field path, but any remains would have been destroyed when the railway company excavated a deep cutting and tunnel in 1855.

From Carey Court a length of overgrown hollow-way lies below the present footpath leading to a picturesque inn, quaintly named The Cottage of Content and formerly the Miner's Arms. From here it follows a scenic riverside road to Hoarwithy, where Boat Meadow is the field which travellers crossed to the 'great boat of the river' at Hoarwithy Passage.

Nearly lost in a maze of lanes lying to the east of Ross, three roads which were turnpiked by the Newent Trust lead through the parishes of Linton, Upton Bishop and Aston Ingham. Before this date other

Newent roads had been maintained by the Gloucester Trust since 1726, and an interesting collection of Mortgages, Securities, Assignments and Leases relating to these roads may be examined at Gloucester Record Office. Two of these routes can be identified from their descriptions in the Newent Road Act of 1802:

> through the several Parishes of *Newent* aforesaid, *Linton*, and *Upton Bishop*, in the County of *Hereford*, to join the said Turnpike Road leading from *Hereford* towards *Newnham*, at a Place called *The Crow Hill*, in the Parish of *Upton Bishop* aforesaid: And whereas the Road leading from the Bottom of *Kilcott Hill*, near a place called *Phillip's Cottage*, in the Parish of *Newent* aforesaid, to the Lea Line in the Hamlet of *Newland*, in the said County of *Gloucester*, and also the Road branching out of the said last mentioned Road near a Place called *Perrin's Wood*, in the Parish of *Aston Ingham*, in the said County of *Hereford*, and passing through a Place called *The Croose Green*, and joining the Road leading from the said Town of *Newent* to the said City of *Hereford*, near the Great Pool on *Gorsley* Common, are in a very ruinous and dangerous State, and cannot be amended, widened, improved and kept in Repair by the ordinary Course of Law:

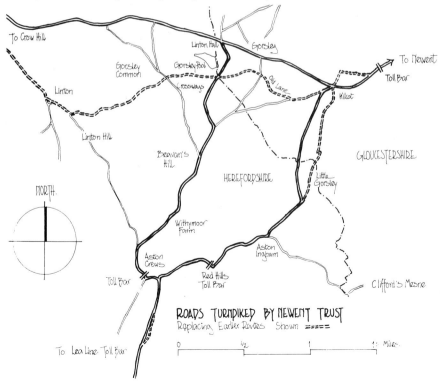

ROADS TURNPIKED BY NEWENT TRUST
Replacing Earlier Routes Shown ═════

The first road forms the B4221 along a straightforward route leading from Crow Hill in Upton Bishop through Gorsley and Kilcot towards Newent. It was an entirely new road opened in 1810, replacing a meandering way leading from Linton across the legendary wilds of Gorsley Common and then along Old Lane to Kilcot. With a good navigator this pleasant but narrowing route can be explored by car.

The second toll road connected Newent with the Hereford to Gloucester highway at Lea Line. It closely follows the line of the present B4222 from Newent to Aston Crews where it continues along a minor road to Lea Line. Between Kilcot and Little Gorsley a realignment was made, leaving behind an interesting stone surfaced road running along a parallel ridge.

The last route was impossible to locate from its details in the 1802 Act as Perrin's Wood was unable to be traced, but a following Act of 1824 added 'to the top of Withymore Pitch'. This together with the help of pre-1802 maps, tithe maps and Ordnance Surveys made it apparent. It must have led from Aston Crews toll bar, past Withymoor Farm, across Old Lane at Crossways and joined the new turnpike road at Gorsley opposite the turning to Dymock and Kempley. Two cast-iron mileposts survive on the Newent – Crow Hill road, one near the County boundary and another opposite Ross Golf Course.

An 18th century basket coach (from Samuel Smiles'
Lives of the Engineers).

5 TRAVELLING THE TURNPIKES

'*The Roads.*—The Roads in this neighbourhood were, but a few years back, remarkably bad, but they are now as good as any in the county. They are under the care of commissioners, who meet at stated times to direct their improvement; and there is a surveyor, whose sole business it is to keep them in repair.'

Ross Guide 1827

Contemporary Descriptions

The turnpike roads of Herefordshire and its borders were well documented by numerous writers, and their impressions provide a fascinating insight into travelling through town and country. William Gilpin wrote in his Wye Tour of 1770 'From Ross to Hereford the great road leaves the river, which is hardly once seen. But it is not probable that much is lost! for the whole country here has a tame appearance'. In 1787 the Hon. John Byng described the road from Gloucester to Ross in his Diaries 'Our road was very good and pleasant thro Huntley, and thro narrow, wooded lanes by the villages of Lea, and Weston, to the town of Ross in Herefordshire, passing near many picturesque scenes – Ross, which we rode violently thro, in a shower of rain, is a well placed, but an ill-paved town'.

From Ross, Byng followed a 'bye course, thro lanes, by the advice of our host, to the ferry near Goodrich, which our horses cross'd without terror'. After investigating the castle he continued along 'A narrow lane of a mile led us into the turnpike road, whereon, for 5 miles, we never exceeded a foots pace, so transcendantly gratified were our eyes with the lofty woods, and the river gliding by us! and particularly with the situation and neatness of the village of Whitchurch ... The road went, often, so near the river, that with the advantage of the hills and views, we fancied our ride to be fully equal to the water journey'.

At the end of the 18th century G. Lipscomb made a journey into South Wales and reported 'The approach to Hereford does not inspire a traveller with any high idea of its consequence, cleanliness, or respectability! the entrance being through a street of wretched and half-falling huts, and between a double row of dunghills placed at their doors. As the road, though not very good, was far from being miry'.

The roads from Monmouth around this time were described by Charles Heath. The turnpike route to Ross 'was always the best road leading from Monmouth for the space of two miles! but Ganarew Hill, with many other parts, were in a dreadful state, being full of large rocks and loose stones, that rendered it dangerous both to horses and foot passengers. Such alterations, however, have since taken place, and are daily going forward, that it is now become the direct post road from London to all parts of South Wales and the South of Ireland'. From Monmouth to Hereford the road 'from the bottom of the hill at the turnpike, as far as the end of the Buckholt Wood, was one continued holloway, ten feet deep near the whole of that distance; while above the road, was a rough stone causeway half a mile long, for the accommodation of foot passengers'.

In his *General View of the Agriculture of the County of Herefordshire* of 1805, John Duncumb reported: 'Much however has been done within the last twenty or thirty years, and a considerable spirit is excited towards promoting further improvement. The late Hon. Mr. Foley, of Stoke, with his accustomed liberality, gave an extent of ground through valuable fields near his house, as the site of a new road ... Mr. Hereford, of Sufton, Mr. Cotterell of Garnons, and many other gentlement, have envinced a similar patriotism'.

While touring the Wye in 1815, Charles Heath visited Marcle Hill where an 'old villager' told him 'when he was a young man, and drove his master's team, he had gone with his wagon from hence to Ledbury, without the wheels turning round, the horses dragging it, by main strength, thro' mud and mire, all the way'. After this encounter Heath returned to Ross along an alternative route 'following a road from Marcle to King's Caple, where a Horse Ferry across the Wye at Hoarwithy opposite, keeps open the communication with the surrounding neighbourhood: from whence a good turnpike road will conduct the visitor by Cradoc to Wilton and Ross; which ride, as here laid down, will embrace nearly all the fine points of the River between that town and Hereford'.

In Heath's *Excursion Down the Wye*, passages of flowing prose describe the toll roads in the Wye Valley during the 1820s. At Pencraig 'from the nature of the soil, the roads soon become dry even after a succession of wet weather', and at Goodrich 'the great turnpike road leading from all parts of South Wales to London, runs thro' the centre of the parish, and several respectable families add to the sociability of the neighbourhood'.

Near the end of the turnpike era, the Rev. Robinson remarks in his *Manors of Herefordshire* that Wormbridge House, pulled down in 1798 'appears to have been a mansion of the Hanovarian type, surrounded by out-buildings and faced by a range of stables so extensive as to suggest that the Herefordshire roads in the last century could not be traversed, except with the aid of abundant horse power'.

Vehicles

Literary gentlemen travelled in relative comfort either on horseback or by post chaise. Riding horses were sturdy, sure-footed cobs capable of covering twenty-five to thirty miles a day as confirmed by William Cobbett in his *Rural Rides* of the 1830s. While making his way to Bolitree near Weston he relates 'I intended to sleep at Gloucester, as I had, when there, already covered twenty-five miles, and as the fourteen, which remains for me to go, in order to reach BOLITREE, in Herefordshire, would make about nine more than either I or my horse had a taste for'. A post chaise was hired by travellers from local innkeepers together with horses and postboys, which were both changed every ten to fifteen miles. According to W.H. Pyne and C. Gray in the early 1800s 'A post-chaise and pair will go 7 or 8 miles an hour with ease' and 'A post-chaise and four, which is travelling in its best style, will go 10 miles at an average'.

Other vehicles to be seen on the Herefordshire toll roads were private carriages which included chariots, berlins, landaus and phaetons together with the public stage, mail or post coach. In 1774 Thomas Pruen from Gloucester started the first post coach service from Hereford to London, advertising his 'New Coach' in the *Hereford Journal*. From the information provided it averaged a speed of only four mph and cost each passenger £1.5s for the long journey. 1794 is a date given for the establishment of a mail coach service in Hereford, but an entry in the *Gloucester Journal* of 1785 offered 'new and Elegant Mail Coaches from London to Gloucester, Hereford and all Parts of South Wales'. Pyne and Gray in 1800 reported 'The mail-coach goes, we believe, at an average, above seven miles an hour, including stoppings, and eight without reckoning them, and with all this rapidity it is so comfortable, that many gentlemen, who have carriages of their own, frequently prefer making journies in it to town.'

In rural Herefordshire during the 18th and 19th centuries there was an increase in the numbers of waggons and carts drawn by horses or oxen. Daily commodities of stone, brick, timber, poles, lathes, lime, coal, corn, hay and manure were conveyed through the turnpikes and along the toll roads. Carriers operated regular freight services from Ross and Hereford carrying assorted goods from food to furniture, which can be read in a carrier's account book of 1826−7 housed at Hereford Library.

Stage waggons were adequately described by W.H. Howse: 'These lumbering covered vehicles, drawn by six or eight horses at an average speed of 2 − 3 miles an hour, took the place of the panniered horses or donkeys of earlier times for the transport of goods by road until supplanted by the railways. The poorer classes of passengers also used them. They reached Kington rather before the coaches. A once-weekly London wagon took nearly a week for the journey. By 1848 there were two wagons each week, connecting at Hereford with wagons from other places.'

A covered waggon of 1802. (W. H. Pyne)

Charles Heath provides another interesting account of waggons using the Monmouth to Hereford toll road:

Such indeed was the narrowness of the road, that to every waggon a boy was attached, as an *avaunt courier*, who preceded the team a considerable way, blowing all the time a large horn, to give notice to those travelling the same line to halt where they could pass with mutual convenience. In addition to the boy's horn, a hoop springing from the collar of the fore horse was fastened, on which were placed five of six large bells;—when in motion, the noise arising from a number of horses thus attired, made the road one continued uproar for many miles; the Herefordshire farmers on this side of the county drawing their supplies of coal and lime from the Forest of Dean. Sometimes a spirit of opposition arose in the minds of these knights of the whalebone whip, who regardless of each other's admonition of approach, proceeded till they came in contact, when *stronger* arguments were appealed to; the consequence of which was, that the weaker party was compelled to put his horses to the tail of the waggon and drag it back for a mile, sometimes two, or till they could pass without further interruption.

Few vehicles survive from this period of travel, but examples can be seen at the Hereford and Worcester County Museum at Hartlebury, and at the Rural Heritage Centre on the Doward, near Ross. In the Transactions of the Woolhope Club, 1960, Winifred Leeds gives a delightful description of the Royal Mail Coaches

'painted in black and maroon, were all of the same design. The door panel bore the royal arms and the name of the route – e.g. London – Carmarthen, while on the outer panels were the royal monogram and the number of the coach. Four passengers could ride inside and three on top – one by the coachman and two behind him. The driver was an employee of the contractor, but the guard was a servant of the P.O. and was provided with a resplendent red coat with blue facings, and a cockaded black hat with gold ribbon. He sat in isolated splendour at the back and was responsible for the safety of the mails. To that end he had a blunderbuss, a cutlass and a brace of pistols to keep off thieves. He also had a horn, sounded to warn slow-moving vehicles to draw aside, or to give toll-gate keepers plenty of time to have their gates open for the coach to gallop through – for it paid no toll.

An 1820s waggon travelling on the road from Ross to Gloucester (H.Lib.)

THE GREEN DRAGON
POSTING COMPANY,
HEREFORD (Limited),

Having taken the Business of Messrs. W. & J. BOSLEY & Co., beg to state that, having made extensive additions to the Stock of Horses and Carriages, and having entirely re-arranged the

POSTING ESTABLISHMENT,

they feel assured that they shall be able to carry on the business to the comfort and satisfaction of the Public.

THE COMPANY ARE PREPARED TO SUPPLY

OPEN OR CLOSE CARRIAGES, OR HORSES, BY THE JOB, OR FOR A TERM;

AND

HEARSES, WITH PLUMES,

AND

MOURNING COACHES,

AT IMMEDIATE NOTICE.

Attention is particularly called to the fact that no Fees will in future be payable to the postboys or drivers, as they will be included in the Charges made by the Company.

It is requested that all orders and communications may be addressed to **Mr. GEORGE WEAVER**, the *Manager of the Company*, at the *Office*,

BROAD STREET, HEREFORD.

Hereford, March, 1867.

Tolls and Gate Keepers

With a few exceptions road users paid at each turnpike gate. From a table of tolls published by the Hereford Trust in the mid 19th century – a traveller on horseback was charged 1½d., and 6d. was taken for every horse drawing a carriage, chaise or coach, but 'any horses or carriages employed for carrying the mails of letters and expresses, under the authority of the Post-Master-General – shall be exempt from payment'. Waggons and carts paid according to the width of their wheels and the contents of their loads. For example 'every Horse, Mare etc. drawing common stage wagons or carts, with broad wheels at each Gate 4d.', and 'For every Horse, Mare etc. drawing timber carriages, with narrow wheels 9d.'. Broad wheeled vehicles caused less damage to the roads, so they paid a cheaper rate.

The collectors were called pikemen, gate keepers or toll collectors, and were obviously disliked by the public. The job attracted unsociable characters portrayed by Charles Dickens in *Pickwick Papers* 'They're all on 'em men as has met with some disappointment in life ... Consequence of vich, they retire from the world, and shut themselves up in pikes, partly with the view of being solitary, and partly to revenge themselves on mankind by takin' tolls'.

Women were also employed as collectors, such as an unsavoury character at Skenfrith. 'An old woman, called a witch, collected toll at the turnpike gate at Norton Cross. There were four roads with three gates, two of them being about forty yards from the toll house. She lived alone and used to come to open the gates in any convenient costume night or day. It is said that, before coming to Norton Cross, she had the care of a toll gate on the Ross Road and there being no house attached, she made her home in a large sugar cask, probably as contented as Diogenes'. Another female collector was Mary Parsons employed by the Ross Trust at Gatsford in 1854. Due to 'Complaints in various respects and of dangerous bites from her dog' she was removed, but before her replacement was appointed, the Trust found it 'necessary to make present dwelling habitable by repairs or by a new wood house'. Later that year £45 was paid for 'new Gatsford Toll House'.

Accidents

Severe weather, inadequate roads, fast driving and drunkenness were the main causes of road accidents during the turnpike age. When

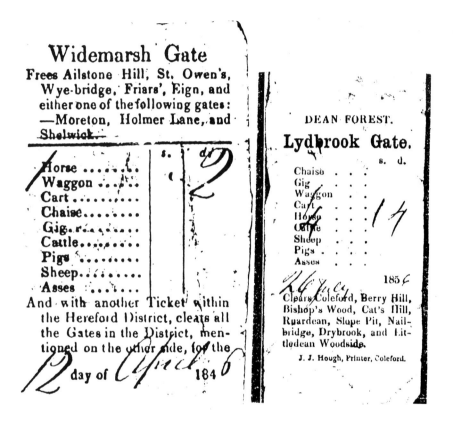

Two surviving toll tickets. (H. Mus./H.Lib.)

coachmen encountered difficulties they instructed their passengers 'First class keep your seat, Second class get down and walk, Third class get down and push'. Drivers had a reputation for drinking, swearing and bad behaviour until the Golden Age of Coaching in the 19th century. At this 'romantic' time they were known to be skilled, immaculate and polite. They generally kept to the left of a highway, a custom dating back to when horsemen kept this side, enabling them to use their sword arm if needed. Some drivers disregarded this tradition which invariably led to unpleasant incidents.

Bad weather caused a couple of accidents experienced by a guard on the Cheltenham, Hereford, Aberystwyth Mail Coach between the years 1838–54. His stories were retold by Mrs. Leeds in 1960:

> Crossing Plynlimmon on a night of dense fog and a blizzard, they lost their way and the coach fell over a 60 ft. precipice. Mercifully, owing to the depth of the snow into which they fell, the driver and guard were not killed, though two of the horses were, and the two inside passengers suffered severely from cuts from the broken glass. Within two hours they managed to right the coach and after a terrible journey succeeded in reaching Cheltenham, just in time to catch the up London mail.
>
> At the time of the great floods in November, 1852, a bad accident befell this coach. Leaving Gloucester about midnight, travelling via Ledbury, it was crossing the Frome Bridge about 4 miles from Hereford when it was precipitated into the swollen river, the bridge having been washed away. Three horses were drowned, but the fourth, and the guard, driver and one passenger escaped. Not so the unfortunate inside passenger, a Hereford solicitor named Hardwick.

Even though the Turnpike Trusts endeavoured to improve the road system, they were repeatedly considered to be in a dangerous condition as reported in Ross Trust's Minute Book. Entries of 1848 record 'dangerous state' of roads at Pencraig and Hoarwithy, which 'should be put in a proper order without a days delay'. By 1837 a total of 4,000 coaches were travelling the turnpike roads of the country, many being driven at excessive paces causing unnecessary accidents, so timid passengers chose to travel by 'the slow coach'.

In 1786 the *Gloucester Journal* was concerned about the effects of alcohol on drivers: 'The number of country people, who have lost their lives within the last six months by going home from markets and fairs in a state of intoxication, has been very considerable in this county; yet the frequency of such accidents makes no impression'. Despite this warning a horrific incident occurred in 1796 'On Friday last an inquest was taken on the body of William Jones, of Lancaut, in this county, Yeoman, by Mr. Joyner, of Berkeley. It appeared that Jones in a state of intoxication, returning home from Chepstow, on Sunday 10th, missed his road in the night, and fell from the high Cliffs that overlook the river Wye, opposite to Piercefield House. The precipice in that place is not less than 50 yards high. The body was not discovered till last Wednesday evening, when some gentlemen and ladies of Chepstow, walking by the river side, discovered it mangled by Vermin in a shocking state'.

In 1843 *The Sunday Times* reported a fatal accident in Hereford:

ST. OWEN'S TURNPIKE GATE.
Overthrowing of the Hereford Mail.—On Saturday evening the mail from Hereford to Cheltenham left the Green Dragon, the wind being very rough, and proceeded as far as St. Owen's *Turnpike gate*, which had been thrown back to allow it to pass. Owing, however, to the want of any fastening, and the boisterous state of the weather, it rebounded just as the leaders got through. The consequence was that the gate caught the near wheel horse, causing the animal to plunge and to break the trace and the near wheel rein. The *gate* rebounded a second time, and the coachman, Mr James Eyles, then lost all command of the very spirited team of horses, which set off at full speed. Whether he jumped off or fell off does not very clearly appear. He was conveyed to the infirmary where he expired at a quarter to 8 o'clock ... The mail was overturned against a bank close to the *gate* leading to the Portfields; and the pole being broken, the leaders were set at liberty, and proceeded towards Tupsley at a furious rate.

An unusual accident at Harewood End in the 1850s was described by John Webb: 'Where the Bierless road falls into the Hereford road, is a pool said to be haunted − teams used to be frightened there at night or run away − one waggoner had his leg broken in the attempt to stop his team − and I am not sure that one was nearly killed from similar causes. Coachmen had very severe difficulties with their horses which used to take fright there. I have passed it late at night on horseback being sent from a baptism at Hoarwithy − but my horses took no notice'.

Road Making

Travelling along the Herefordshire roads in the 18th and 19th centuries were journeys of discomfort. In 1805 Duncumb reported that roads were made or repaired with 'Coarse limestone, properly broken', and by 1815 parish surveyors in Herefordshire were directed to mend their roads with 'rubble or refuse stone' plus 'materials from waste grounds, rivers and brooks' together with 'stones, or other materials from any land, not inclosed'. This quality of road building did not improve till the appearance of two Scotsmen − Thomas Telford and John MacAdam.

These experienced and gifted engineers with their new technology made a contribution towards the improvement of Herefordshire's roads. Telford's associations with Ross has already been discussed. His building skills can be admired at Over near Gloucester, where his beautifully designed bridge of 1830 is now redundant, but preserved as an ancient monument. MacAdam's cheaper methods of road construction were popular with many Trusts. His son Loudon surveyed roads for Ledbury, Bromyard and Abergavenny Trusts during the 1820s and 30s.

Road materials used by the Ross Trust were obtained from quarries at Bishops Wood, Coppet Wood and Lydbrook. They were conveyed by barge along the Wye and delivered at 'Kerne Bridge for Walford Road, Glewstone for Monmouth Road, and at Wilton for Hereford and Hoarwithy Roads'. The quarries are shown on early 6″ Ordnance Sheets, but now disused and overgrown, they are not easy to locate. The best ones to investigate are those on Coppet Hill, where they lie adjacent to public roads and footpaths. Remaining cobbled roads can be examined at Ledbury, Much Marcle, Chepstow and Llangattock near Crickhowell.

Itineraries and Maps

Early travellers needed to find their way along inadequately sign-posted routes, relying on local knowledge from innkeepers. Since 1675 Ogilby's Britannia was available, showing roads on a series of strip maps. His survey was based on the statute mile, which although had been introduced in 1593 had been slow in replacing the local or customary mile, which varied from 2035 to 2500 yards. A hundred years passed before Daniel Paterson produced his masterly itinerary of Roads in Great Britain. It ran into twenty-one editions and became the standard road book, providing a wealth of information. An enlarged and improved edition, edited by Mogg informs the reader

'The plan of the present edition is simply this: it is an attempt, as far as the nature of the work will allow, to Map the ground; and so closely has it been acted upon, and faithfully followed, that instead of meeting with seats, as heretofore, mixed up in one confused and heterogeneous mass, they now succeed each other, with very few exceptions, arranged in the precise order in which they occur upon the road; and thus, in this part of the work, it will, I trust, be readily admitted, has a great improvement been attained. The turnpike gates and bridges, objects in themselves imposing upon every road, are here given in a form calculated to impress upon the traveller a more correct idea of his relative situation than would probably occur to the most intelligent, from the simple notice of the name of a river, or the more imperfect substitute of the letters T.G.'

Paterson's 18th edition includes lists of Direct Roads, Cross Roads and Country Seats followed by tables of Population, Counties and Charges for Post Horses plus some finely engraved maps. With turnpikes, bridges, inns and mileages recorded in the text it provided a dependable guide for 19th century travellers. With the formation of the Ordnance Survey in 1791 and an advancement in surveying techniques, map makers such as Cary, Smith, Greenwood, Walker and Teesdale were able to produce more accurate maps. These, with early Ordnance Survey sheets and county maps of Taylor, Price and Bryant provide a contemporary record of Herefordshire which can all be examined at Hereford Library.

Inns

With an increase in travel and transport along the mail and coach routes, modest ale-houses blossomed into larger coaching inns and post-houses offering rest and refreshment to the weary traveller. The stable yard presented a busy scene, with impatient horses waiting to be changed and harnessed. These facilities were available at inns at Ross, Monmouth, Ledbury, Hereford and Gloucester as well as at smaller establishments in the countryside.

However, in 1781 the Hon. John Byng was not impressed with the Beaufort Arms at Monmouth 'I arriv'd here this evening, rather tired, and am now sitting in a mean room at this bad inn; which may be the best here. The stables are new and good, that's a comfort; for if my horse does not fare and sleep well, well there wou'd be an end of my travel'.

The *Ross Guide* of 1827 reported 'The principal inns in Ross are — the Swan, which keeps Post Chaises, and Horses for hire, and from which the London and South-Wales Coaches set out. The King's

Opposite: *an unusual itinerary from Paterson's Roads of 1828.*

CROSS ROADS

ALRESFORD to PETERSFIELD.

	From Petersfi.	*From*	*From Alresf.*	
	14	* *ALRESFORD,* *Hampshire, to*		
ALRESFORD, at Old Alresford, Old Alresford House, Lord *Rodney*; Upton House, Hon. Col. *Onslow*; The Parsonage, Rev. *F. North*; and 3 m. distant, Armsworth House, *J. T. Villebois*, Esq.	$12\frac{3}{4}$ $11\frac{1}{2}$ $6\frac{1}{4}$	Bishop's Sutton Ropley Dean 🖼 *to Alton 7 m.* To the Gosport Road 🖼 *to Alton* $6\frac{1}{4}$ *m.* *To Bishop's Waltham* $11\frac{1}{2}m.$ *To Fareham* $19\frac{1}{4}$ *m.* *To Gosport* $24\frac{3}{4}$ *m.*	$1\frac{1}{4}$ $2\frac{1}{4}$ $7\frac{3}{4}$	THE GOSPORT ROAD, $1\frac{1}{2}$ m. distant on right, Basing Park, *Richard Norris*, Esq.
THE GOSPORT ROAD, 1 m. distant, Rotherfield Park, *James Scott*, Esq.	$2\frac{1}{2}$ $1\frac{3}{4}$	Stoner Hill Steep	$11\frac{1}{2}$ $12\frac{1}{4}$	STONER HILL, 2 m. distant, Borden House, *H. Chawner*, Esq.; and farther to the right, Langridge Lodge, — *White*, Esq.
STONER HILL. Ashford House, *C. Alderson*, Esq.	$12\frac{1}{2}$	* *PETERSFIELD* *OR,* * *ALRESFORD,* *Hampshire, to*	14	PETERSFIELD, 1 m. distant, Nursted House, Gen. *Hugonin*.
	9	Bramdean * *PETERSFIELD,* *page 593*	$3\frac{1}{2}$ $12\frac{1}{2}$	

BATH to HEREFORD, BY NYMPHSFIELD, NEWNHAM, MITCHEL DEAN, AND ROSS.

	From Hereford	*From*	*From Bath*	
	$59\frac{1}{2}$	* *BATH, Somersetsh., to* Junction of the Roads, *Gloucester., page 361*	$19\frac{1}{2}$	
	40	🖼 *to* King's Cote, *Hunter's Hall*		
JUNCTION OF THE ROADS, Lasborough Park, *S. P. Paul*.	$38\frac{1}{4}$	$\frac{1}{4}$ *m. farther,* *to Wotton under Edge 4 m.*	$21\frac{1}{4}$	BATH, Prior Park, *W. Thomas*, Esq.; and Crow Hall, — *Tugwell*, Esq.
		🖼 *to Dursley* $3\frac{3}{4}$ *m., thence to Berkeley 5 m.* *to Purton Passage* $10\frac{1}{4}$ *m.*		
NYMPHSFIELD, 2 m. distant, Stouts Hill, Rev. *W. L. L. Baker*.	37 35¼	Turn 🚧 pike *To Minchin Hampton* $5\frac{1}{4}$ *m.* 🖼 Nymphsfield	$22\frac{1}{2}$ $24\frac{1}{4}$	KINGSCOTE is the seat of Col. *Kingscote*.
	33	*About* $\frac{1}{4}$ *m. farther,* 🖼 *to Dursley 4 m.* *To Minchin Hampton* $5\frac{1}{2}$ *m.* 🖼 * Frocester	$26\frac{1}{2}$	
FRAMPTON COURT is the seat of *H. C. Clifford*, Esq.	$30\frac{3}{4}$	Church End, *Junction of the Road* *to Berkeley 7 m.* 🖼 *to Bristol* $24\frac{1}{4}$ *m.* *to Dursley* $5\frac{1}{2}$ *m.*	$28\frac{3}{4}$	NYMPHSFIELD, Woodchester Park, Lord *Ducie*.
	29	$\frac{1}{2}$ *m. farther,* *Forward to Gloucester* $8\frac{1}{2}$ *m.* 🖼 *to* Frampton Court	$30\frac{1}{2}$	

Head, at which Post Chaises and Horses are also let out. The George, at which is held the Excise Office'. Then, in 1837, James Barrett opened his Royal Hotel, purpose-built to meet the demands of the coaching age. His hotel staff in 1851 comprised 'milliner, bar maid, waiter, chambermaid, under waiter, kitchen maid, boots, two house-keepers, and a hostler'.

At Ledbury in 1787 Byng was again disappointed. 'At 4 o'clock I arrived at Ledbury; and dined there, in haste, on some tough mutton

Former Inn at Hoarwithy.

chops; a sad inn; and well that I had not made it my night stop.' Improvements were made, and 80 years later the Feathers and Royal Oak were described as 'two good hotels and posting houses'. While in Hereford Byng stayed at the New Inn 'a house of noise and bustle'; this, together with the Redstreak Tree and the Swan and Falcon, were the principal coaching inns, in the 18th century city. W.H. Howse in 1946 adds 'The Redstreak Tree (presumably named after the apple introduced into Herefordshire by the first Viscount Scudamore in the 17th century) fronted High Town from where is now the Market Hall; it appears to have been the most important inn during the greater part of the 18th century. The New Inn went on longer and coaches started there up to the 1830's; it stood at the corner of Widemarsh and Maylord Streets, on the site now occupied by the Corporation gas Showrooms. Towards the end of the 18th century the Green Dragon came into prominence, and remained an important coaching station to the end, most coaches after 1850 starting there.'

In Gloucester the Bell and King's Head were recommended by Paterson in 1828; these replaced an earlier establishment, now known as the New Inn, which still provides a vivid example of a former coaching inn. Others to visit are the Royal and King's Head at Ross, the Green Dragon at Hereford, the Walwyn Arms at Much Marcle, the Bell at Skenfrith, the George at Newent, the Crown at Whitchurch, the Green Man at Fownhope and the Harewood End Inn. Since the coaching age a number have closed such as the Anchor at Fownhope, the Old Harp at Hoarwithy, the Broad Oak and Southwell Arms at Garway and the Old Gore at Foy.

Roadside Craftsmen

Thousands of horses nationwide drew coaches, carriages and waggons along the turnpike roads. This required dependable and skilled blacksmiths, saddlers, wheelwrights and coach builders to keep things on the move. In 1859 Gloucester boasted sixteen blacksmiths, five wheelwrights, eight saddlers and five coach-builders, while Hereford listed ten smiths, six wheelwrights, seven saddlers and three coach-builders.

Villages like Fownhope had their own saddler and harness maker, farrier, blacksmith and wheelwright. James Bailey ran an extensive wheelwright's business during the mid 19th century. His sons also shoed horses and made broad-wheeled carts and waggons.

Insignificant places situated at cross roads, such as Crow Hill and Broad Oak, became important enough to offer the services of a blacksmith and wheelwright. By 1867 over a dozen men were employed in Ross shoeing horses, making harness, mending wheels and constructing coaches. By that date the Hereford, Ross and Gloucester Railway was well established, being opened in 1855.

Although these roadside craftsmen played an essential role in transport and communication, few records exist. Most villages had forges, reminders of which can still be seen at Walford, Mordiford, How Caple, Much Marcle, Sellack, St. Weonards, Weston under Penyard, St. Owen's Cross and Harewood. Tools of the trades with fully equipped workshops or forges can be inspected at the National Waterways Museum at Gloucester Docks and the Rural Heritage Centre on the Doward at Whitchurch.

St. Owen's toll gate, dismantled by the Hereford Trust in 1869/70.
(W. Collins)

6 END OF AN ERA

'The Coaching Age was dead; the glory had departed from the high roads. The coach-proprietors, the mail- and stage-coaches, the post-chaises, the post-boys, the coachmen and guards, the busy ostlers and stable-boys, the cheery innkeepers and bustling waiters found most of their occupation gone. The turnpikes were being removed: by 1870 few were left round London, since they were not worth the salary paid to the pike-keepers. The prophets were saying that in another fifty years the roads would be grass-grown from London to Edinburgh. Through the second half of the nineteenth century the railways were supreme.'

Jane Oliver 1935

With the rapid development of railways and a changing political climate the turnpike roads became increasingly obsolete. Since the establishment of the turnpike system there had been certain dissatisfaction at their results, although at their height 1,000 trusts had been formed to maintain 22,000 miles of roads. Although they committed many errors and were much maligned, they did make a significant contribution to road improvements. It was probably the best system possible at that time, as expressed in the Webb's classic *Story of the King's Highway*:

The Turnpike Trust and its toll was, in short, the only way open. Without the local initiative and local support fostered by the thousand separate Trusts; without the emulation and mutual instruction which their several experiments promoted; without the large revenues which the toll drew from the multitudinous but politically helpless road users, no considerable improvement in the highways of England would have taken place for, at any rate, the first three-quarters of the eighteenth century, and very little would have been achieved before the passing of the Reform Bill.

A minor incident recorded by Thomas Vaughan in 1833 perhaps indicated a resentment that later exploded in South Wales. It was at Byford, near Hereford, that 'One little bit of mischief occurred, I well remember, when we had arrived opposite to the fifth mile-post; one of our party, not having a wholesome fear of the Turnpike Trust floating before his mental vision, picked up a large stone and hurled it at the upper part of the post with such force as to strike the cross-board free from its fixture, and send it spinning far into the field beyond'.

The unpopularity of the toll roads in South Wales led to an uprising called the Rebecca Riots named after a verse in Genesis. Riots took place during the 1840s including this incident at Glasbury gate in 1843, described by H.T. Evans: 'The posts were sawn off about half a yard above the ground, and the gate, after being sawn in two and otherwise mutilated, was thrown into the River Wye. The old woman who collected the tolls saw only three men employed, and they told her to keep quiet, as they would not injure her. About fifty persons were secreted near the place, to be of assistance if necessary.' Men disguised as women caused such havoc by continually destroying gates and toll houses, resulting in at least one murder when 'A woman pikekeeper who was rash enough to declare that she recognised the assailants of her gate, was deliberately shot dead'. The government was forced into holding an Inquiry in 1844 which formed the South Wales Trusts into County Roads Boards.

This attempt to abolish toll roads spread into Herefordshire, where a more silent rebellion took place in the production of passive pamphlets. One was by Mr. Morris Sayce from Kington in 1844.

WHEN I first heard of the appointment, by Her Majesty, of Special Commissioners to enquire into the grievances of South Wales, the origin of which grievances, and the subsequent insurrectionary actions of the Rebeccaites, was the unreasonable number of Turnpike Gates erected by various Turnpike Trusts, and the consequent exorbitant demand for Tolls, it immediately occurred to me that a plan of a less objectionable character might be devised for raising money to keep the Turnpike Roads in proper repair; I have subsequently reflected much upon the subject, knowing that the grievance was not confined to South Wales alone, but extended over the major part of the Kingdom.

Another, writing in 1863 proposed, 'The improvement I suggest consists in abolishing all Turnpikes, and in providing for the repair of the Roads by a Rate upon property, on the principle of the Poor-rate'.

For one hundred and fifty years the toll roads of Herefordshire had rung to the sound of iron on stone, horse-drawn vehicles carrying

A former toll house at Copse Cross in Ross. (Heather Hurley)

loads of coal, lime, timber, gravel, turnips, potatoes, straw, corn, bricks, poles, lathes and cider and the shuffling of oxen, cattle, hogs and sheep being driven to market. Then in 1853 this 'tedious, uncertain and expensive conveyance' was revolutionised. The first steam railway reached the county.

The railway companies were quick to promote the benefits of rail travel and transport, as advertised in this early Prospectus of 1836:

The farmer will have a good and cheap communication with all the Manufacturing districts of England, his produce will be within twelve hours' reach of London; fat beasts now reaching Smithfield in a lame and impoverished state, losing from eight to twelve per cent. in weight, will be brought to market in a good and wholesome condition. To the Traveller the advantage of locomotive power is acknowledged; the formation of such a communication with Herefordshire will be the means of inducing many thousands who have not enjoyed the beauties of scenery in the neighbourhood of Ross and Windcliffe, to resort to that great attraction so wonderfully blended by nature.

Great excitement and a blaze of publicity attended the opening of the Hereford, Ross and Gloucester Railway in 1855. The *Hereford Times* reported:

At length we have the intense satisfaction of being able to record the long wished for event which has brought our city and county into direct communication with the Metropolis. After many anxious years of hope deferred, Herefordshire sees itself united, by three links of iron, to the vast railway system which has done so much, and promises so much more, for the advancement of civilization. Although united by the Shrewsbury and Hereford line to the great hive of manufacturing industry in the North; shaking hands, by means of the Newport, Abergavenny and Hereford line, with the busy mining community of South Wales, and thus replaced in its former position, on the high road between South Wales and Liverpool, Herefordshire still lacked that ready communication with the Metropolis which is essential to the prosperity of every province; it still felt the need for free access for its products to the greatest mart in the world; still needed the spur to intellectual, social, and commercial activity, which a close connection with London alone can supply.

The arrival of the railway did not appear as a threat to the Ross Turnpike Trusts. They remained neutral on this subject with one of their trustees, James Wallace Richard Hall, serving as solicitor and secretary to the Hereford, Ross, Gloucester Railway Company, and liasing between the two parties. Before the opening of the Ross to Monmouth Railway the *Ross Gazette* of 1872 printed:

'It is confidently expected that after the Ross and Monmouth Railway is opened for traffic (as it will be in the course of the present year), whereby the roads numbered 2 and 7 in the Act will be relieved from their present heavy coal traffic; that the annual sum of £1,000 will be sufficient to keep the roads in a proper state of repair; but if it be not; it is urged that the Trustees, under the discretionary powers which it is submitted they have under section 30 of the Act, ought to expend a sufficient portion of the income of the Trust in repairing the roads, and leaving them, when the time shall come for throwing them upon the district, in an efficient state of repair.

'It has been proved that the existence of a railway has not diminished the income of the Trust; for, since the opening of the Hereford, Ross, and Gloucester Railway, the income has been as high as it was previously, the income lost being replaced by that produced by the increase from tolls for light vehicles, which cause but little wear and tear to the road.'

Minor alterations were made to the toll roads during the construction of the railways, where bridges interfered with roads, as at Dinedor and Lea. On the Gloucester road in 1853 the Ross Trust minuted that the Railway Company 'would allow the trust to rebuild a toll house at Hownhall. The house to be a convenient cottage with Privy and Pigsty. To command three different roads'. At Tudorville a former stretch of the Ross to Monmouth line is now preserved as the Betzdorf Walk.

After the government's attempt at reforming road administration in South Wales, an Act was passed in 1862 to set up Highway Boards in England. It united parishes into Districts run by waywardens and surveyors. By 1865 the shires of Hereford, Gloucester and Monmouth were formed into Highway Districts including Ross in 1863, a year after their final 'Turnpike Roads Act'.

During the 1860s and 70s parliamentary legislation enabled trusts to hand over their roads to Highway Districts. Many trusts were in financial difficulties at a time when their Road Acts were due for renewal. From a Statement unexpectedly discovered in a roll of Quarter Sessions, the Ross Trust is shown as solvent in 1870. The gross income was £2438 which surprisingly revealed an increase from £2324 in 1868. The Hereford Trust was already in debt by 1862, although their revenue from tolls amounted to £6281. Nationwide the Turnpike Trust accounts of this period were published in the *Times* of 1867:

The annual abstract recently issued of the accounts of Turnpike trusts in England and Wales shows that the revenue from *Tolls*, was £1,025,631 in 1865. The value of *Statute Duty* performed, and the parish composition in lieu of *Statute Duty*, with incidental receipts and £7,373, money borrowed, brought the *Toll* income of 1865 up to £1,102,203. The expenditure of that year was £1,098,975; of which £655,011, nearly 60 per cent. went in maintenance and improvement of the roads, more than 7 per cent. in salaries, nearly 2 per cent. in law charges, 27 per cent. in paying off debt and paying interests, 4 per cent.

in incidental expenses. In 1864 the bonded debt was reduced to £4,046,346; and unpaid interest to £456,707. The debt paid off is for the most part paid at a discount, the mean amount of the discount being about 25 per cent.; the usual course when money is in hand is stated to be to pay off the creditor who will for that sum discharge the largest amount of debt.

As each Act appeared for renewal the government recommended:

> in which cases the Trusts should be allowed to come to and end, and in which cases, and subject to what conditions, a further term should be granted. The policy of this Committee, which was that of the House of Commons rather than that of the Cabinet, was decidedly in favour of winding up as many Turnpike Trusts as possible; and of conceding a renewal only where the financial position of the Trust or the circumstances of the locality made such a renewal almost irresistible.

This was the method described by the Webbs. Between 1867 and 1878 a series of 'Annual Turnpike Acts Continuance Acts' covered Herefordshire, either extending or extinguishing the relevant trusts.

The Ross District Highway Board Minute Book illustrates the last stages of a turnpike trust. From 1870 its committee discussed the 'extinction of the Trust', 'that the roads shall be charged upon the Common Fund of the Highway Board', and the Trust should 'place roads in such a state of efficiency to make burden of their future repairs as light as possible'. In 1872 an entry reads 'agreed by all members that roads in a wretched state of repair in many places', and in the same year the *Ross Gazette* announced the proposed discontinuance of the Ross Turnpike Trust as follows:

THE REPAIR OF THE TURNPIKE ROADS.
Captain Power said that some two or three months ago, he was sorry to say, a decision had been come to by the Ross Turnpike Trust Commissioners to apply to the Home Office for permission—(as the mortgage upon the tolls was nearly paid off)—to allow the trust to cease on and after the 1st January next. The permission had been granted, and the whole of the turnpike roads in the district would have to be thrown upon the Highway Board for their maintenance, and the cost drawn from the ratepayers in the various parishes, which would entail upon them a very heavy burden. This he regretted very much, because the roads were in a bad state, and, if the Commissioners had been willing to have gone on with the trust for a longer period, there was no

The Dry Arch, Goodrich.

W. B. R.

doubt that some equitable arrangement would have been made, by which the burden would have been more fairly distributed upon the public generally and those who made use of the roads.

As the matter stood at present, the whole of the burden would fall upon the shoulders of those who used the roads the least, and such being the case there was no help for it but to do the best they could. He found upon inquiry that the Turnpike Commissioners had now no funds derivable from tolls for the repair of the roads, because the money so obtained was appropriated to pay off the mortgage. It appeared to him, too, that the roads at the present time were in an exceedingly imperfect state. In fact, on most of the roads in the Ross Turnpike district the metal was nearly worn through, and the ruts in some places were so deep that it was with great difficulty a carriage could be got along.

This being so, it was necessary that something should immediately be done to repair them, for if they allowed the matter to stand over till January, when the Trust would cease, the roads would be in such a bad, pulpy state, that in hauling materials to repair them they would be cut through to such an extent that it would cost a great deal more money to repair the damage thus done than it would to put the roads in order at the present time.

Although wide coverage was given of the town's 'Proposed Abolition of Turnpike Roads', no reports have been traced in local papers regarding the demise of the Hereford Trust. Only one brief mention appeared in the *Hereford Times* on 24th October 1868, reporting a 'strong argument against the abolition of Turnpikes'. At the end of the year the Trust issued its final statement of account. But the Whitchurch and Llangarron District of Turnpike Roads did not cease until 1875.

By 1871 Hereford and Ledbury had abolished their toll roads, with Ross following on 1st January 1873, Newent in 1874, and Gloucester and Monmouth in 1878. Most trusts had ceased by 1888 when a Local Government Act transferred the responsibility of main roads to newly formed County Councils. But it was not until 1895 that the very last turnpike road came to an end, between Shrewsbury and Holyhead.

Today, all that remains of the turnpike age are a few toll houses, occasional milestones or mileposts, some road realignments and one or two purpose built roads with their typical twists and turns. These together with surviving documentation remind us of a vital, but nearly forgotten, development in the history of our highways.

SOURCES

Select Bibliography

Addison, Sir W, *Old Roads of England*, 1980
Albert, W, *Turnpike System in England*, 1972
Bick, D, 'The Enigma of Holloways,' *Glos. Local History Bulletin* No. 52, 1985
Bird, A, *Roads and Vehicles*, 1969
Brenchley, D.R, and Shrimpton, C, *Travel in the Turnpike Age*, 1968 (University of Newcastle)
Byng, Hon. John, *The Torrington Diaries* 1781–1787
Cave, Brian, *Weston and Lea*, 1982
Copeland, J, *Roads and their Traffic*, 1968
Cross, A, *Old Industrial Sites in Wyedean*, 1982
Duncumbe, J, *General View of the Agriculture of Herefordshire*, 1805
Fosbroke, Rev. T.D, *The Wye Tour*, 1833
Gloucestershire Directory, 1859
Gloucestershire Turnpike Roads, G.R.O., 1973
Heath, Charles, *Excursion Down the Wye*, 1828
Heath, Charles, *Monmouth*, 1804
Herbert, N, *Road Travel and Transport*, 1985
Hereford Turnpike Roads, anon., 1863
Herefordshire Directories, 1858, 1867, 1902
Jervoise, E, *Ancient Bridges of Wales and Western England*, 1936
Mogg, E, *Paterson's Roads*, 1829
M.N.J., *Bygone Days in the March Wall*, 1926
Oliver, Jane, *The Ancient Roads of England*, 1936
Parnell, Sir H, *Treatise of Roads*, 1833
Paterson, D, *Roads in Great Britain*, 1778
Pawson, E, *Transport and Economy*, 1977
Reader, W.J., *MacAdam*, 1980
Richards, J, *Stagecoach*, 1976
Richardson, C, *Driving*, 1985
Richardson, J, *The Local Historian's Encyclopedia*, 1974
Ross Guide, anon, 1827
Searle, M, *Turnpikes and Toll-Bars*, n.d.
Smith, Peter, *The Turnpike Age*, 1970 (Luton Museum)
Strong, Dr. G, *Handbook to Ross*, 1863
Taylor, C, *Roads and Tracks of Britain*, 1979
Trotter, A.W, *The Dean Road*, 1936

Turner, J.H, *Herefordshire Countryside Treasures*, 1981 (Hereford & Worcester C.C.)
Tweed, Rev. H, *Wilton Castle*, 1884
Waters, Ivor, *Turnpike Roads*, 1985
Watkins, A, *Early British Trackways*, 1922
Watkins, A, *The Old Straight Track*, 1925
Watkins, A, *Old Standing Crosses of Herefordshire*, 1930
Webb, S and B, *Story of the Kings Highway*, 1913

Journals and Newspapers Consulted
Gloucestershire Notes and Queries
Hereford Record Office Friends Newsletter
Hereford Tracts
Notes on Gloucestershire History
Ross Civic Society Newsletter
Transaction of the Woolhope Naturalists' Field Club
Hereford Journal, Hereford Times, Ross Gazette

Road Acts Consulted
Ledbury, 1721, 1793
Gloucester to Hereford, 1726, 1768
Hereford, 1730, 1749, 1769, 1789, 1810, 1819, 1835
Ross, 1749, 1773, 1791, 1815, 1862
Monmouth, 1755, 1831
Magor, 1758
Crickhowell, 1772, 1793, 1814, 1833
Abergavenny, 1831
Newent, 1802

Other Acts
Highway, 1555
Turnpike Continuance, 1868
Local Government Boards Highway, 1879
Mordiford Inclosure, 1809
Kerne Bridge, 1825
Hoarwithy Bridge, 1855
Holme Lacey Bridge, 1857

Archives

Note H.R.O. = Herefordshire Record Office
G.R.O. = Gloucestershire Record Office.
Aconbury Gate Accounts, 1801, H.R.O.
Buckle, E, Study of the Parish of Dinedor, 1964–7
Estimate of Hereford Turnpike Trust, 1843, H.R.O.
General Statement of Hereford Turnpike Trust, 1844, H.R.O.
General Statement of Ross Turnpike Trust, 1829 H.R.O.
Gloucester and Hereford Railway Prospectus, 1836
Gloucester and Hereford Turnpike Trust Minute Book, 1726–1768, G.R.O.
Hereford Turnpike Account, 1781
Hereford Turnpike Tolls, c1850

Improvement at Perrystone Hill, 1825, H.R.O.
Quarter Sessions, Mich. 1820, 1829, Trinity 1871, H.R.O.
Ross Highway Board Minute Book, 1863–1875, H.R.O.
Ross Turnpike Trust Minute Book, 1838–1854, H.R.O.
Sale of Old Road and Toll House at Wilton, 1795 H.R.O.
Schedule of Turnpike Acts, G.R.O.
Schedule of Turnpike Returns, 1820, H.R.O.
Telford's Report on the Mail Road, mss., 1825
Telford's Report on the South Wales Mail Road, 1825, G.R.O.
Walford Gate Toll Ticket, 1856
Webb, Rev. J, Pengethley and Scudamore Papers, c1850
Widemarsh Gate Toll Ticket, 1846

Maps

Rees, W, Map of South Wales and the Borders in the 14th century, 1922
Ogilby, J, Britannia, 1675
Taylor, I, Herefordshire, 1754 (1 mile: inch)
Andrews, J, A New Map of England and Wales, 1786 (c6½ mile: inch)
Paterson, D, Itinerary, 1787
Cary, J, Herefordshire, 1787, 1793, 1804
Smith, C, Herefordshire, 1801
Price, Henry, Herefordshire, 1817 (1 inch: mile)
Ordnance Survey, first edition, 1831 (1 inch: mile)
Bryant, A, Herefordshire, 1835 (1½ inch: mile)
Walker, J, Herefordshire, 1843
Ordnance Survey, Pathfinder Sheets, 1040, 1041, 1064, 1065, 1087, 1088 (1/25,000)
Ordnance Survey, Landranger Sheets 148, 149, 162 (1/50,000)

Plans

Survey of Cross Farm, 1699, H.R.O.
Survey of the River Wye at Bridstow, 1788, H.R.O.
Plan of New Road from St. Weonards, 1809, H.R.O.
Plan of Road from Wormelow Tump, 1809, H.R.O.
Plan of Road from the Quern, 1815, House of Lords R.O.
Plan of Turnpike Road from Monmouth, 1818, H.R.O.
Over Ross and Black House Estates, 1818, H.R.O.
Plan of Road between Old Forge and the Lea, 1822, H.R.O.
Plan of New Road at Goodrich, 1824, H.R.O.
Telford's Plan Old Forge to Huntley, 1824, H.R.O.
Telford's Plan of the South Wales Mail Road, 1824, G.R.O.
Plan of the Turnpike Road between Ross and Ledbury, 1833, H.R.O.
Plan of Road avoiding Dock Pitch Hill, 1833, H.R.O.
Plan of Turnpike Road from Hereford to Ross, 1834, H.R.O.

INDEX

Bold type denotes an illustration